The Life and Death of
CRAZY HORSE

The Life and Death of CRAZY HORSE

by Russell Freedman

Drawings by Amos Bad Heart Bull

Holiday House/New York

Copyright © 1996 by Russell Freedman
ALL RIGHTS RESERVED
Printed in the United States of America
FIRST EDITION

Library of Congress Cataloging-in-Publication Data
Freedman, Russell.
The life and death of Crazy Horse / by Russell Freedman ; with
drawings by Amos Bad Heart Bull. — 1st ed.
p.   cm.
Includes bibliographical references and index.
Summary: A biography of the Oglala leader who relentlessly resisted
the white man's attempt to take over Indian lands.
ISBN 0-8234-1219-9 (hardcover : alk. paper)
1. Crazy Horse, ca. 1842–1877 — Juvenile literature.   2. Oglala
Indians — Biography — Juvenile literature.   3. Oglala Indians — Kings
and rulers — Juvenile literature.   4. Oglala Indians — Wars — Juvenile
literature. [1. Crazy Horse, ca. 1842–1877.   2. Oglala Indians —
Biography.   3. Indians of North America — Biography.]   I. Bad Heart
Bull, Amos, 1869–1913, ill.   II. Title.
E99.03C72214   1996   95-33303   CIP   AC
978'.004975'0092 — dc20
[B]

Source of drawings is cited on page 163.

For Jacob

Contents

The Main Characters

CRAZY HORSE, called "Curly" as a boy
WORM, his father, originally known as Crazy Horse
GATHERS HER BERRIES, his stepmother
LAUGHING ONE, his older sister
LITTLE HAWK, his younger brother
BLACK SHAWL, his wife
THEY-ARE-AFRAID-OF-HER, his daughter
BLACK ELK, his younger cousin

OLD-MAN-AFRAID-OF-HIS-HORSES, Oglala chief
YOUNG-MAN-AFRAID-OF-HIS-HORSES, Old Man's son
RED CLOUD, Oglala chief
JACK RED CLOUD, Red Cloud's son
BLACK BUFFALO WOMAN, Red Cloud's niece
NO WATER, Black Buffalo Woman's husband

HUMP, Oglala warrior, Crazy Horse's *kola*, or best friend
HE DOG, Oglala warrior, comrade of Crazy Horse
LONE BEAR, Oglala warrior, comrade of Crazy Horse
SHORT BULL, Oglala warrior
RED FEATHER, Oglala warrior

LITTLE KILLER, Oglala warrior
LITTLE BIG MAN, Oglala warrior
AMERICAN HORSE, Oglala warrior

CONQUERING BEAR, Brulé trade chief
SPOTTED TAIL, Brulé warrior and chief, uncle of Crazy Horse
LITTLE THUNDER, Brulé chief
SITTING BULL, Hunkpapa war chief and holy man
WHITE BULL, Hunkpapa warrior
GALL, Hunkpapa warrior
TOUCH-THE-CLOUDS, Miniconjou warrior and chief
BLACK KETTLE, Cheyenne chief
TWO MOONS, Cheyenne chief
OLD BEAR, Cheyenne chief
WOODEN LEG, Cheyenne warrior
YELLOW WOMAN, Cheyenne survivor at Blue Water Creek

LIEUTENANT JOHN L. GRATTAN, killed with his men at the "Grattan Massacre"
GENERAL WILLIAM S. HARNEY, called "Mad Bear" by the Sioux
COLONEL WILLIAM O. COLLINS, commander at Fort Laramie
LIEUTENANT CASPAR COLLINS, son of William Collins, friend of Crazy Horse
COLONEL JOHN M. CHIVINGTON, commander of the Colorado militia
COLONEL HENRY B. CARRINGTON, commander of troops on the Bozeman
    Trail
CAPTAIN WILLIAM J. FETTERMAN, killed with his men at the "Fetterman
    Massacre"
GENERAL WILLIAM TECUMSEH SHERMAN, commander of the U.S. Army

Lieutenant Colonel George Armstrong Custer, commander of the
Seventh Cavalry Regiment, called "Long Hair" by the Sioux

Major Marcus A. Reno, Seventh Cavalry Regiment

Captain Frederick Benteen, Seventh Cavalry Regiment

General George Crook, called "Three Stars" by the Sioux

Colonel Nelson A. Miles, called "Bear Coat" by the Sioux

Lieutenant William H. Clark, military commander at Red Cloud Agency

Lieutenant Jesse Lee, government agent at Spotted Tail Agency

Lieutenant Colonel Luther P. Bradley, commander at Camp Robinson

1

The Strange Man of the Oglalas

He was a little boy running barefoot through the village when the first wagon trains traveled west along the Oregon Trail. His people, the mighty Teton Sioux, had never been conquered. The biggest and strongest Indian nation left in the United States, the Sioux ranged far and wide across the high plains in search of fresh game and the camps of their rivals.

By the time Crazy Horse reached full manhood, his people had been swept up in a desperate struggle to remain free. Pressed on all sides by growing numbers of invading whites, they fought to save their hunting grounds and their way of life.

This terrible conflict between whites and Indians on the Great Plains was just beginning when Crazy Horse was growing up. A shy, sensitive youth, he rose to fame as the greatest of all Sioux warriors, a leader who believed that nothing was more important than freedom. He never signed a treaty with white men, and he resisted them all his life.

As a boy he had a powerful vision. He found that if he trusted his vision, he could never be hurt by the arrows and bullets of his enemies. And while he was a fearless fighter, even reckless in combat, his sacred vision seemed to

Sioux warriors wearing clothing of different seasons.

protect him. Among the Crows, the Indian enemies who knew him best, it was said that Crazy Horse had a magical gun, a medicine gun, that hit whatever it looked at, and that he himself was bulletproof.

His own people knew him as "Our Strange One," and at times, he seemed very strange indeed. He wore no war paint, took no scalps, and refused to boast about his brave deeds. A quiet loner, he would walk through the village lost in thought or ride out on the plains to be by himself. His fellow

Sioux loved to dance and sing, but Crazy Horse never joined a dance, not even the sun dance, and they say that nobody ever heard him sing.

When he was still a boy, grown-ups often discovered him standing in the shadows, listening to their conversation. When he grew up, he continued to listen. "He never spoke in council and attended very few," said his friend He Dog. "There was no special reason for this, it was just his nature. He was a very quiet man except when there was fighting."

Even his appearance set him apart. He was a small man for a fighter, with a wiry frame, soft brown hair, and pale skin. "Crazy Horse had a very light complexion, much lighter than the other Indians," Short Bull remembered. "His features were not like those of the rest of us. His face was not broad, and he had a sharp, high nose. He had black eyes that hardly ever looked straight at a man, but they didn't miss much that was going on all the same."

As far as we know, Crazy Horse never allowed himself to be photographed. Dr. Valentine T. McGillycuddy, the post surgeon at Camp Robinson, Nebraska, tried to persuade the Sioux warrior to pose for his camera, but Crazy Horse always turned him down. "My friend," Crazy Horse would ask him, "why should you wish to shorten my life by taking from me my shadow?"

Many details about Crazy Horse's life remain uncertain or unknown. Much of our information about his personal life and character comes from interviews conducted more than fifty years after his death. In 1930, two writers, Eleanor Hinman and Mari Sandoz, traveled through Sioux country in a Model T Ford. They interviewed Crazy Horse's surviving friends and relatives, old-timers such as He Dog, Red Feather, Short Bull, and Little Killer, men who had lived with Crazy Horse and fought beside him. Even though these ancient warriors were recalling events from long before, their memories were sharp and they did not often disagree. All of them described

Crazy Horse as unusually quiet and reserved, not boastful like most Sioux warriors, and they agreed that he was like that as a youth. Thanks to these and other interviews, and to the written accounts of white men who came into contact with Crazy Horse, writers and historians have been able to reconstruct the story of his life.

Crazy Horse's people, the Teton or Lakota Sioux, were divided into seven independent tribes—his own Oglalas, and their relatives the Brulés, Hunk-

Battle scene.

papas, Miniconjous, Two Kettles, Sans Arcs, and Blackfeet. These tribes, in turn, were made up of small hunting bands. At one time, the Tetons had lived far to the east, in the woodlands around the headwaters of the Mississippi River. Pressed by Chippewas armed with the white men's muskets, they gradually migrated westward to the Missouri River and beyond.

Pushing aside weaker tribes, the Sioux spread out across the plains, where the buffalo, in herds many millions strong, turned the grasslands black with their numbers. The Sioux roamed as far west as the Yellowstone River and its major tributaries, the Powder, Tongue, and Bighorn. This wild and beautiful country was also claimed by the Crow Indians, who became the Tetons' chief rivals. During generations of conflict with the Crows, the Sioux allied themselves with the Northern Cheyennes.

By Crazy Horse's time, a new wave of migrants was beginning to sweep westward. This time the newcomers were white people. Like the Crows before them, the Sioux were confronted with a powerful threat to their hunting grounds and freedom. As white miners, ranchers, and farmers streamed into the West, it was the clear duty of the United States Army to protect the advancing frontier, and the Indians stood in the way.

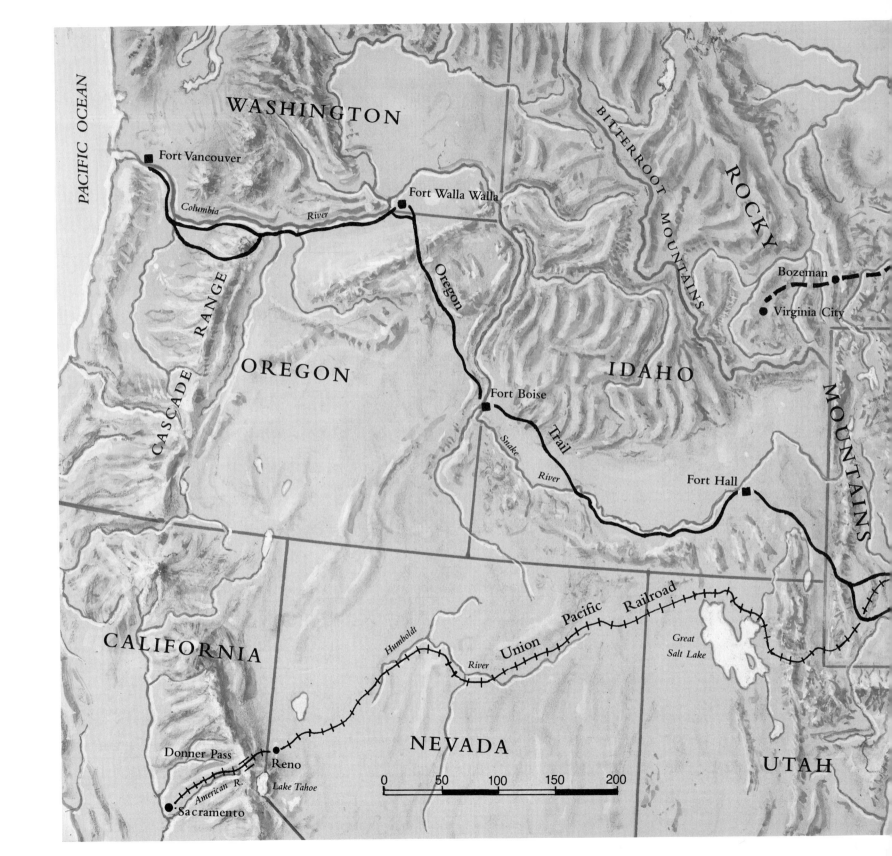

PACIFIC OCEAN

WASHINGTON

Fort Vancouver

Fort Walla Walla

Columbia

River

CASCADE RANGE

OREGON

BITTERROOT MOUNTAINS

ROCKY

Bozeman

Virginia City

IDAHO

Oregon

Fort Boise

Snake

Trail

River

Fort Hall

MOUNTAINS

CALIFORNIA

Humboldt

Union Pacific Railroad

River

Great
Salt Lake

NEVADA

Donner Pass

Reno

UTAH

American R.

Lake Tahoe

Sacramento

0   50   100   150   200

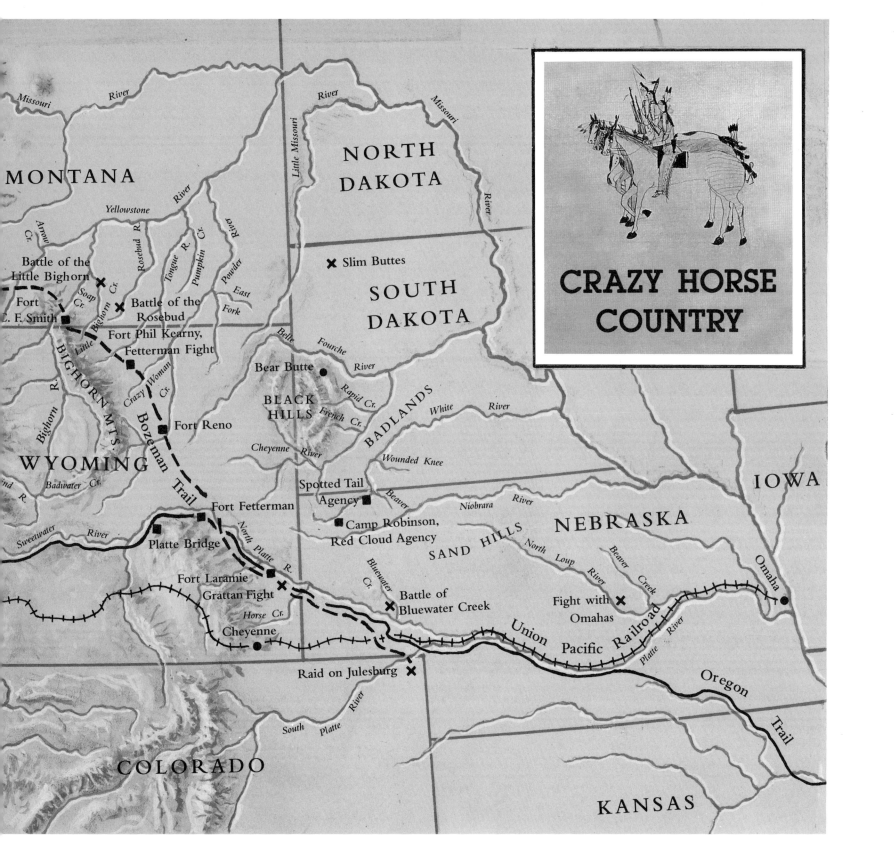

MONTANA

Missouri *River*

Yellowstone *River*

Arrow Cr.

Rosebud R.

Tongue R.

Pumpkin Cr.

Powder River

East Fork

Battle of the
Little Bighorn ✕

Fort
C. F. Smith ■

Soap Cr.

Bighorn Cr.

Little Bighorn R.

✕ Battle of the
Rosebud

Fort Phil Kearny,
Fetterman Fight ■

BIGHORN MTS.

Crazy Woman Cr.

Bozeman Trail

■ Fort Reno

Bighorn R.

WYOMING

Wind R.

Badwater Cr.

Sweetwater River

■ Fort Fetterman

■
Platte Bridge

North Platte R.

■ Fort Laramie
✕ Grattan Fight

Horse Cr.

Cheyenne ●

NORTH
DAKOTA

Little Missouri River

Missouri River

River

✕ Slim Buttes

SOUTH
DAKOTA

Belle Fourche River

Bear Butte ●

BLACK
HILLS

Rapid Cr.

French Cr.

BADLANDS

White River

Cheyenne River

Wounded Knee

Spotted Tail
Agency ■

■ Camp Robinson,
Red Cloud Agency

Beaver

Niobrara River

SAND HILLS

Bluewater Cr.

✕ Battle of
Bluewater Creek

NEBRASKA

North Loup River

Beaver Creek

Fight with ✕
Omahas

IOWA

Omaha ●

Union Pacific Railroad

Platte River

Raid on Julesburg ✕

South Platte River

Oregon
Trail

COLORADO

KANSAS

CRAZY HORSE
COUNTRY

2

Curly

He was born at a Sioux encampment on Rapid Creek, in the shadow of the tall and beautiful Black Hills. His mother held him in her arms and sang a soft lullaby, a growing song of the Plains Indians, to help make her baby son straight-limbed and strong.

If he started to cry, she caught his tiny nose between her thumb and forefinger, and with her palm held gently against his mouth, stopped the crying. That is how he learned the first and greatest lesson of his life: no one, not even a newborn infant, could be allowed to put the people in danger. A single cry could guide a roving enemy to the village, or scare off game during a hunt.

The date of his birth is uncertain. According to his boyhood friend Chips, it was the year of the Big Horse Steal, when the Oglala Sioux captured a hundred horses from their enemies, the Shoshonis. As the white folks reckoned time, that was the year 1841.

Even as a little boy he seemed different from the other Sioux children. People would remember him as a strangely serious youngster, quiet and thoughtful. And he was set apart by his looks—his narrow face, light skin, and soft curly hair. Emigrants traveling the Oregon Trail through Sioux territory sometimes mistook him for a captive white boy.

His own people called him the "Light-haired Boy," or most often, "Curly." He would not receive his grown-up name until he performed a noteworthy deed or had a memorable dream.

Crazy Horse—*Tasunke Witko*—was the name of Curly's father, and before that, his grandfathers. In the Lakota language the name means "Holy, Mystical, or Inspired Horse"—a horse that can perform extraordinary feats.

Curly's father was an Oglala holy man, a dreamer and a prophet respected for his wisdom and good advice. His mother, whose name has been lost to us, came from another Sioux tribe, the Brulés. She died when Curly was still very young. Her place in the lodge was taken by her sister, Gathers Her Berries, who raised the children of Crazy Horse as her own. Curly had an older sister, Laughing One, and a younger brother, Little Hawk.

Like any other small Sioux child, he was petted and fussed over by all of his relatives, and by every member of his family's band. Toddling about the village, he was free to explore as he pleased. He could wander into any tipi, where he would be pampered and fed. Every cooking pot would have a little extra for a hungry boy. Every grown-up would be happy to hear his tales of the day's adventures.

Curly's father played with him for hours on end. Crazy Horse's big hands would reach out for the little boy, sweep him high off the ground, and plant him firmly on his shoulders. Curly would grab his father's braids, one in each hand, like reins. He would hang on for dear life, screaming with delight, as his father made the "Tchlch" sound that started horses moving, and went prancing around the tipi.

▶▶9◀◀

He was never touched by a punishing adult hand. The Sioux did not believe in spanking or whipping a child. "We never struck our children, for we

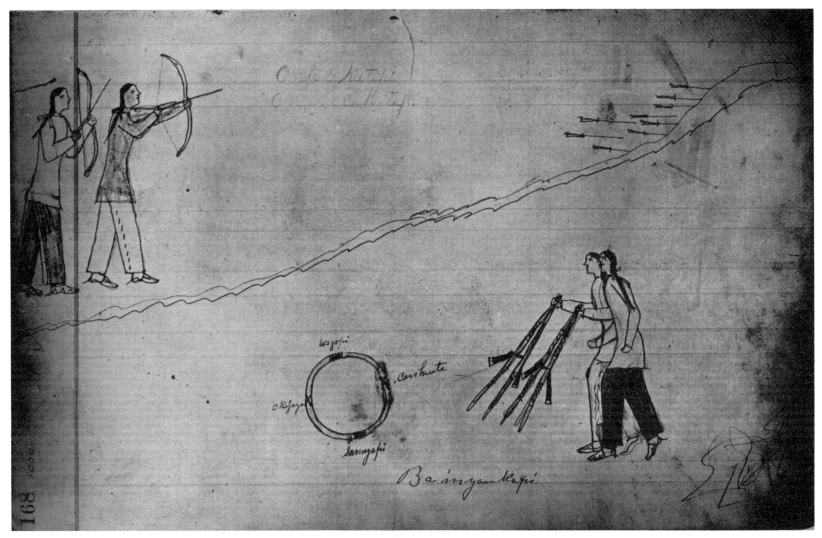

Two games: "shooting their best" and "chasing the hoop."

loved them," a Sioux woman recalled. "Rather we talked to them, gently, but never harshly. If they were doing something wrong, we asked them to stop."

▶▶10◀◀ As Curly grew up, his father coached him in the thousand and one skills he would need to live a free life on the plains — how to ride, how to hunt, how to fight. Crazy Horse made the boy's first bow and arrows, and taught him how to use them. From then on, shooting arrows was a major pastime. Curly practiced with other boys his age, competing in games to see who could shoot the farthest, the fastest, the straightest. Before long he was making his own bows. When he grew older, he could hold a fistful of arrows in his left hand and shoot them so quickly that the last arrow was on its way before the first one touched the ground.

When he was old enough to straddle a horse, his father gave him a colt of his own that he could ride to his heart's content. He learned to mount on the right side, holding his bow in his left hand when he leaped on, leaving his right hand free to draw the bowstring fast. Riding bareback, he would gallop across the prairie under the endless sky, lashing his eager little pony to full speed, clinging only with his knees, shouting and laughing for pure joy. He learned how to maneuver a speeding pony, how to leap from one horse to another, how to gallop past a fallen comrade, reach down, and pull him up onto the back of the horse. And he learned to understand his pony's habits and needs. At night he took his turn with other boys guarding the village herd, keeping watch for horse thieves.

Sioux boys never tired of pony races and footraces. They held endless running, jumping, and wrestling contests, and competed in rough-and-tumble games that tested their strength, their endurance, and their willingness to suffer pain without complaining. In the fire-throwing game, teams of boys would attack each other with flaming sticks until one of the teams retreated. "In close fighting after you have hit an enemy two or three times, your torch goes out," one player remembered. "Then you get your share until his stick dies out."

Many of the boys paired off in close, lifelong friendships. They became *kolas*, pledging to help and protect each other in every undertaking, to share equally in all things. Curly's *kola*, his special friend, was an older boy named

High Back Bone, or Hump. The two youngsters went everywhere together.

Growing up on the high plains, the boys learned to watch and listen, to observe everything that happened around them. They learned the names of the birds and the meanings of their calls, the habits of creatures big and small. They knew how to study the sky and see a change in the weather, how to put an ear to the ground and hear the distant rumble of hooves, how to find their way across the treeless plains without getting lost. Every living thing, every tree and blade of grass, the streams and lakes, the heavens and all they contained—all had lessons to teach, and all were sacred, part of *Wakantanka,* the Great Mystery, the spiritual force that existed in every form of life.

Like other boys their age, Curly and Hump idolized the warriors of their village—those brave young men who rode off in war parties and came home with enemy horses and scalps. Those men were the heroes of the tribe. Returning from an expedition, they paraded through the village on painted ponies, singing war songs, wearing flowing crests of eagle's feathers and bright robes fringed with the scalp locks of their enemies. All of them had bows and arrows at their backs, some carried tall lances with iron points that flashed in the sunlight, and one or two might be armed with guns.

As each warrior passed, the women of the village called out his name to honor his bravery. Excited children ran whooping and screaming beside the horses and followed the parade. At the victory dance that night, everyone sat in a great circle around a roaring fire. One after another, the homecoming warriors, their faces painted black as a sign of victory, stepped into the circle to sing war songs and tell about their brave deeds. The people cheered each man for what he had done. And small boys like Curly gazed at the warriors with eager wonder and admiration, dreaming of the day when they, too, would return from an expedition and ride triumphantly around the village.

Returning from a successful war expedition, warriors gallop around the village.

3

Council at Horse Creek

Once or twice a year, Curly's people visited the white men's trading post at Fort Laramie on the North Platte River. They raised their tipis outside the fort's stockade walls and traded buffalo robes for muskets and gunpowder, iron kettles, steel knives, needles, blankets, tobacco, and all sorts of other luxuries and modern conveniences.

So tempting were the white men's goods that some Oglala bands took to living near Fort Laramie the year round. Curly's people—the Hunkpatila band—kept their distance, visiting the fort only when they wanted to trade. They referred scornfully to their relatives as the "Hang-Around-the-Forts" or the "Laramie Loafers."

Fort Laramie was a busy way station on the Oregon Trail, which followed the Platte River westward toward the Rocky Mountains, cutting through the heart of buffalo country and the southern hunting grounds of the Sioux. Emigrants had been traveling along the trail in their covered wagons since the summer of 1841, bound for the rich farmlands of Oregon.

At first the Sioux had raised the hand of friendship to the white people passing through their country. The emigrants were allowed to go on their way in exchange for gifts of coffee, sugar, and biscuits, which the Indians prized. It became an established custom that the emigrants would offer to feed all Indians who came around to visit. The whites were not always happy about this, but handouts of food were better than trying to fight their way across the plains.

The emigrants did not stop on their journey except to rest and hunt. But as their numbers increased, the Indians became uneasy. Each year the wagon trains grew longer. Wagons with white canvas tops stretched for miles along the trail, creaking and swaying as they moved through clouds of choking dust.

The only trees on the plains grew along rivers and streams. As the emigrants cut those trees for their cooking and heating fires, the Indians watched cottonwood groves, where they had camped for generations, disappear. Grass in the valleys was eaten down to the ground by the emigrants' cattle. Buffalo and antelope grew scarce in that part of the country as hunters from the wagon trains rode far out on the plains.

In the eyes of the Indians, the whites took the best campsites, devoured the timber and grass, and scared off the game. And there were boastful and arrogant men among them, Indian haters who seemed to be looking for trouble.

Some of the older Sioux knew of the disasters that had befallen Indian tribes east of the Missouri River, wherever white men had moved in and claimed the land. At night around the village campfires, tribal elders told stories about those native peoples in the East who had been crushed and dispossessed, forced off their land and into exile.

As tensions increased, the Sioux began to talk about keeping the whites out of their country. Now and then, hot-blooded young warriors would raid a wagon train, terrifying the emigrants and driving off their horses and cat-

Driving off horses.

tle. And yet the Indians could not stop the endless stream of wagons moving year after year through their hunting grounds. And they could not agree on a course of action. They grew frustrated arguing among themselves about what to do about the white intruders.

Many of the warriors regarded the whites as a distinct and growing danger. But tribal leaders like Old Smoke and Conquering Bear, the so-called trade chiefs, warned against any threat to the supply of trade goods that made life so much easier for the Sioux. They did not want to drive away the white men's trading posts.

Some Oglalas wanted to remain friends with the whites; others became increasingly fearful and hostile. Curly's father brooded about the plight of the Sioux, about the quarrels and disagreements that had divided the Oglalas. And he worried that the traders and their whiskey would destroy the Sioux unless they threw off the white men's influence in their daily lives.

Along with coffee and sugar, the whites had introduced alcohol into Sioux country—*mini wakan,* the Sioux called it, "the water that makes men foolish." For years, white traders had exchanged liberal amounts of whiskey for Indian hides and fur. Alcohol was a profitable item of trade, and all too often, an easy means of taking advantage of the Indians. Many a drunken Indian lost the fruits of his winter hunt when a sober frontiersman tricked him out of his goods. The wiser tribal leaders kept the whiskey wagons out of their camps. Except for a few favored traders, they avoided all contact with the whites.

Curly saw the influence of the whites at close range when his people went down to Fort Laramie to trade. Some Indians traded their horses, their clothing, anything they owned, for whiskey. Drunken quarrels and brawls broke out among the tipis and sometimes spread through an entire camp. Societies of warriors called *akicitas* policed the camps and kept order. They dealt harshly with troublemakers and often drove them from the camp. But the troubles persisted. There were too many loafers and weaklings hanging around the forts, taking the white men's liquor and causing fights. And some of the traders were hard-drinking roughnecks who cheated the Indians every chance they had.

Women's clothing.

In 1849, emigrants on the Oregon Trail were joined by thousands of fortune hunters heading for the newly discovered gold fields of California. Now the unending lines of white-topped wagons stretched from horizon to horizon. More than fifty thousand travelers passed through Fort Laramie that year. The traffic was so heavy that the buffalo fled far to the north and south of the Oregon Trail, never to return to the middle prairies.

By year's end, most of the Indians wished that they had scattered, too. The forty-niners had carried with them an epidemic of cholera that swept across the plains, killing nearly half the Cheyenne tribe and causing terrible losses among the Sioux. Curly's people fled north, trying to escape from cholera country. When they reached the White River, they discovered a Sioux ghost camp, its lodges filled with dead people.

The cholera was followed a year later by a smallpox epidemic. By the time the disease had spent itself, the Indians were in an angry and unforgiving mood. The Sioux and Cheyennes blamed the whites for the epidemic. Some of them believed that white men had deliberately introduced the disease among the Indians, and they talked darkly of revenge. Warriors stepped up their raids on wagon trains and trading posts until, finally, terrified whites appealed to the government for protection.

In 1851, government agents sent runners out to all the Indian tribes in the region, promising plenty of food, guns, and other gifts if they would come down to Fort Laramie for a great peace council. Curly was about ten years old when his band traveled to the meeting that summer. He must have been thrilled, for he had never seen so many people from so many different tribes all gathered together in one place.

Some ten thousand Indians came to Fort Laramie, the largest assembly of its kind that had ever taken place on the plains. Friends and foes camped peaceably near one another—Cheyennes from the Powder River country, Oglalas, Brulés, and other tribes belonging to the Teton Sioux, and those old enemies of the Sioux, Crows from the Yellowstone River and Shoshonis from beyond the Bighorn Mountains, along with Arapahos, Assiniboins, Arikaras, Mandans, and Hidatsas. Many of these people had never met before except in battle.

The tribes competed with one another as hosts, showing their generosity by holding big feasts. Around the night fires, dancing, drumming, and singing went on until dawn. People visited back and forth, youngsters raced their ponies, teenagers flirted, warriors paraded about and exchanged war stories. Curly had a chance to ride his pony from one tribal encampment to the next, meeting boys from distant tribes he had only heard about, speaking to them in sign language.

Warriors on parade.

The tribes were camped around Fort Laramie for nearly a month before the wagonloads of food and gifts that had been promised finally arrived from the East. By then, the gigantic pony herd had cropped all the grass around the fort. The whole encampment moved thirty-seven miles east to a new site at Horse Creek.

On the 8th of September, a booming army cannon announced the opening of the Horse Creek Council. Many tipis had been joined together to form a single large council lodge. In the center of the lodge, buffalo robes were spread on the ground as seats for the government commissioners and the chiefs representing the various tribes. Behind the chiefs, warriors in full ceremonial dress arranged themselves according to their tribes and bands. The leather walls of the council lodge had been rolled up to accommodate the overflow. Pressing the warriors from the rear, the old men, women, and children formed a dense mass of absorbed spectators. Curly was there that day, standing on tiptoe, excited by the spectacle, craning his neck so he could see and hear everything that was happening.

The commissioners and chiefs passed a peace pipe from one to the other, each man taking several puffs. Then the superintendent of Indian Affairs, David D. Mitchell, stood up to speak. He had come all the way from Washington, D.C.

Mitchell told the chiefs that the Great White Father in Washington (the president) wanted to establish a lasting peace on the plains, a peace between the United States and all the independent tribes, and a peace among the tribes themselves. The Indians must allow white emigrants to travel safely along the Oregon Trail, he said. And the tribes must promise to stop making war on one another.

For each tribe, boundaries would be established, and that tribe would have the exclusive right to hunt within its own territory. Finally, the government wanted to build roads and forts to protect the emigrants. In return, the United States promised to provide the Indians with annuities—yearly gifts of food and supplies—for a period of fifty years. Mitchell also pledged that soldiers manning the government forts would safeguard the rights of the Indians against the whites.

For days afterward, the elders of each tribe held their own councils. Curly listened in the background as his father and other Oglala leaders talked about the government's proposals. It was hard to take some of those proposals seriously. The idea of drawing boundaries on a map to separate long-time foes seemed very strange to the Indians. As hunters, they had to follow the buffalo herds wherever they found them. As warriors, their pride and self-respect, their standing in the community, rested on daring horse raids and courageous battle deeds against their enemies.

What were these boundaries drawn across the wide prairie? At the peace talks, the Sioux had objected to the way the government had defined their territory. "You have split my land and I don't like it," Chief Black Hawk complained. "These lands once belonged to the Kiowas and the Crows, but we whipped those nations out of them, and in this we did what the white men do when they want the lands of the Indians." In reply, the commissioners assured the Sioux that the boundaries were only guidelines, and that no tribe surrendered its rights to land claimed outside of its own borders.

But the oddest proposal was the government's demand that the Sioux name a single head chief to speak for all of them. The tribal elders shook their heads and tried to explain that there could be no such thing as a "head" chief over all the Sioux tribes and bands. Indian society was not that simple. Each of the Teton Sioux tribes, and every small band within those tribes, had its own leaders. Those men met as equals in their tribal councils. They shared their authority. Besides, a "chief" inspired loyalty because of his wisdom, his accomplishments, and the force of his personality. He could advise but not command. He could not *order* his people to do anything. If the people lost faith in him, he was no longer their leader.

The Sioux told the government commissioners that one chief could never speak or act for all the Oglalas, or all the Brulés, much less the entire Teton Sioux nation. But Commissioner David Mitchell insisted. And when the tribal leaders could not agree on a head chief to represent them, he picked one for them. He selected Conquering Bear, an easygoing trade chief of the Brulés, who was known to be friendly to the whites.

Conquering Bear was presented with a gold-braided U.S. Army General's uniform and a gilt sword. He became the first chief to "touch the pen" and allow his name to be signed to the Fort Laramie Treaty of 1851. A number of other chiefs picked by the commissioners also signed, but most of them knew it would be impossible to live by the treaty's terms.

Afterward, as the great Indian encampment at Horse Creek began to break up, Curly's people headed north for a buffalo hunt and to settle down for the winter. From that time on they called the Oregon Trail the "Holy Road," because the whites traveling on it were not to be touched.

4

Trouble on the Holy Road

Curly was a quiet boy but a daring one. By the time he was ten or eleven, he had joined a tribal hunting party and killed his first buffalo. He had watched so many hunts from the sidelines, been coached so often by his father and uncles, that when the big day came, he knew just what to do.

He waited with other hunters until the marshals in charge gave the signal. Then he galloped forward, riding without stirrups or saddle. Holding his bow in his left hand, urging his eager pony on with the whip strapped to his right wrist, he picked out a young bull in the stampeding herd. The bull's short tail was erect and his tongue was lolling out from his foaming jaws as he kicked up dust and tried to get away.

Closing in, Curly dropped the rein on his pony's neck and pulled an arrow from the otter-skin quiver at his shoulder. Guiding his pony with his knees, he pulled back the bowstring, aimed for a spot just behind the bull's ribs, and let the arrow fly. It struck with such force that it almost disappeared into the bull's side.

Shouting at the top of his voice, Curly shot another arrow, then another.

Chasing the buffalo.

The bull wheeled around and jumped at the boy's pony. Curly clung to his seat like a leech as his pony twisted and dodged, leaping away from the bull's horns. He could see the bull's eyeballs glaring through his tangled mane, the blood flying from his nostrils and mouth. The shaggy beast sprang once more, then collapsed in a heap into the tall grass.

Not long afterward, Curly showed off his riding skills again when he

Taking the hide off.

joined a group of boys on a horse-catching expedition. They found a herd of wild horses, drove them until the animals tired, then moved in and caught some with rawhide ropes. Curly was the first boy to mount and break one of the wild horses. When they all returned to the village, he was leading his newly captured pony.

His father was so proud that he led Curly around the village, singing the boy's praises, calling out to everyone that he was throwing away his son's old name and giving him a new one. From now on he would be known as His-

Horse-on-Sight. But the new name didn't stick. Everyone continued to call him Curly.

Curly's people still spent most of the year hunting north of the Platte River. Every summer they went down to Fort Laramie, where thousands of Sioux gathered to collect the government annuities that had been promised at the Horse Creek Council. For the time being, the Indians and the whites observed an uneasy truce. Wagon trains rumbled across the plains, watching for trouble and sometimes finding it.

High-spirited young warriors harassed the travelers almost as a sport. Swooping down on wagon trains, they frightened the emigrants into giving them presents, drove off horses and cows, and sometimes slipped into camp at night to spirit away an iron cooking pot or maybe a rifle. Then they galloped off, yipping and yelling on their swift painted ponies. It was great fun, and the emigrants were an easy mark. They did not try to pursue the thieves, as the Crows or Shoshonis would have done.

Conquering Bear and his fellow peace chiefs did what they could to hold their young men back, but the warriors boasted that they were strong enough to drive the whites off the plains whenever they chose. At the same time, some of the army officers stationed at Fort Laramie were itching to get at the Indians. They felt confident that they could whip those unruly Sioux and teach them a lesson they would never forget.

Growing resentment and suspicion on both sides led to senseless outbursts of violence. At Fort Laramie during the summer of 1853, a Sioux warrior asked a soldier for a ride across the Platte River in a skiff being used as a ferry. The soldier refused to take him. In anger, the warrior fired an arrow at the skiff as it crossed the river to the opposite bank.

The next day, twenty soldiers were sent out to arrest the warrior. In the confusion that followed, someone fired a gun. The soldiers replied with a volley of shots, killing five Sioux. Then they hurried back to the fort without their prisoner.

Emigrants passing through the region were greatly alarmed, fearing that the Sioux would retaliate against them. "The Indians no longer look smiling, but have a stearn solumn look," one emigrant wrote in her diary. "We feel this evening that we are in danger."

A few days later, Sioux warriors struck in revenge, attacking an emigrant camp near the fort and killing a family of four. Then the soldiers marched out of the fort and attacked the first Indians they met, killing one and wounding another.

Conquering Bear managed to calm the warriors and smooth things over. After collecting their annuity goods, most of the Indians went north for their fall hunt. When they returned to Fort Laramie the following year, trouble erupted again.

As usual, several thousand Sioux were camped near the fort that summer, waiting for the yearly distribution of food and supplies. Curly was visiting his relatives at a big Brulé encampment just east of the fort. One afternoon a party of Mormon emigrants came rolling down the trail. As they approached the Brulé village, some warriors rode over to scout the caravan and get the settlers to part with a little coffee and sugar.

Just then, a cow bolted from the wagon train. The animal's owner chased it to the edge of the village, but when he saw a big crowd of Indians, he drew back and returned to his wagon. After he left, a Miniconjou warrior named High Forehead, who was visiting in the Brulé camp, shot the cow and the Indians butchered it for its meat.

When the wagon train reached Fort Laramie, the cow's owner stormed into the fort and complained that the Indians had stolen his property. He demanded that something be done. The fort's commander, Lieutenant Hugh B. Fleming, sent for Conquering Bear, whom the whites had appointed head chief of all the Sioux.

Conquering Bear offered to pay for the butchered animal. It was an old cow, he pointed out, and lame besides. It never would have made it across the mountains. Even so, he was willing to pay ten dollars for the animal, twice what it was worth, or else a horse from his personal pony herd. When the angry emigrant demanded twenty-five dollars, the negotiations broke down.

Lieutenant Fleming insisted that the cow killer be turned over to him. That wasn't possible, Conquering Bear replied. High Forehead was a guest in his village. If Fleming wanted to arrest him, he would have to do it himself.

The next morning, Fleming dispatched an arrest party headed by John L. Grattan, a brash young second lieutenant fresh out of West Point. Grattan had never seen the Sioux in battle, but he was positive that they were no match for the U.S. Infantry. More than once, he had boasted that he was eager to "crack it to the Sioux." He had been known to strut about the fort, shaking his fist at Indians, calling them cowards, warning them to look out.

Grattan set out for the Brulé village with a detachment of twenty-nine soldiers, two howitzers, and an interpreter named Auguste Lucien, who had been drinking heavily. Lucien rode about, shouting that all the Sioux were going to be killed, and that he, Auguste, would cut out their hearts and eat them for breakfast. The Indians detested Lucien. They had asked many times to have him replaced.

As the soldiers approached the village, they were met by Conquering Bear and several other tribal leaders. By now, Lucien the interpreter was roaring drunk. Hurling insults and threats at the astonished Indians, he demanded the surrender of High Forehead.

Curly had joined hundreds of other Indians in the bluffs above the village. He watched from afar as the Sioux chiefs faced the blue-coated army officer under the midday sun, while the interpreter shouted and waved his arms.

A long parley took place. Conquering Bear went back and forth between the soldiers and his camp, where High Forehead refused to give himself up. Exactly what happened next will never be known. The facts were lost that morning in a swirl of dust. At some point, the soldiers leveled their guns and fired into the Brulé camp. Caught in the first volley, Conquering Bear fell to the ground, mortally wounded.

In an instant, enraged warriors poured out of tipis and down from the bluffs, swarmed over the soldiers, and took their revenge. When the dust settled, Lieutenant Grattan, his men, and the interpreter lay dead. The lieutenant's body had been pierced by twenty-four arrows.

Curly had seen everything. He had watched in horror as Conquering Bear was cut down by the soldiers' bullets, his mouth gushing blood, and as the soldiers fell under a barrage of arrows and spears. He had seen warriors drag the interpreter out of a nearby tipi, where he was hiding, kill him with war clubs, and mutilate his body.

That afternoon, the entire Sioux encampment around Fort Laramie pulled up stakes. Carrying their wounded chief on a horse-drawn travois, a leather frame slung between two trailing poles, the Indians fled across the plains. They were heading toward the Sand Hills of present-day Nebraska. Curly rode with his stepmother's people, her band of Brulés.

One evening, when the Brulés stopped to make camp, Curly caught a glimpse of Conquering Bear as he was being carried into his tipi. Shaken by

Moving camp. The pack horse is pulling a travois.

the sight of the dying chief, who looked so wasted and ghostly, the boy leaped on his pony and rode out on the prairie alone. He hobbled his horse beside a small lake, climbed a hill, stretched out on the ground, and gazed at the night sky.

He was about thirteen now, and he wanted to seek a vision. Sioux boys his age often went by themselves to some lonely place where they could commune with the sacred powers, hoping for a vision that would guide and inspire them for the rest of their lives. Usually, a holy man helped a boy prepare for his vision quest. The youngster would fast, purify himself in a sweat lodge, and listen to the holy man's advice and instructions before finally setting out.

Curly had gone out impulsively, without the proper preparation, without telling anyone. Stripped to his breechcloth, he lay on the hilltop, staring at the stars. He had placed sharp stones between his toes and piles of pebbles under his back to keep from falling asleep. He would force himself to stay awake and fast until a vision came. He would try to enter the spirit world, the

Seeking a vision.

world that exists behind this one, where there is nothing but the spirits of all things.

For two days he remained on the hilltop without eating, fighting off sleep, his eyes like burning holes in his head, his mouth as dry as the sandhills around him. When he could barely keep his eyes open, he would get up and walk around and sing to himself. He grew weak and faint, but no vision came to him. Finally, on the third day, feeling unworthy of a vision, he started unsteadily down the hill to the lake where he had left his hobbled pony.

His head was spinning, his stomach churning. The earth seemed to be shaking around him. He reached out to steady himself against a tree. Then—as he himself would later describe it—he saw his horse coming toward him from the lake, holding his head high, moving his legs freely. He was carrying a rider, a man with long brown hair hanging loosely below his waist. The horse kept changing colors. It seemed to be floating, floating above the ground, and the man sitting on the horse seemed to be floating, too.

The rider's face was unpainted. He had a hawk's feather in his hair and a small brown stone tied behind one ear. He spoke no sounds, but Curly heard him even so. Nothing he had ever seen with his eyes was as clear and bright as the vision that appeared to him now. And no words he had ever heard with his ears were like the words he seemed to be hearing.

The rider let him know that he must never wear a war bonnet. He must never paint his horse or tie up its tail before going into battle. Instead, he should sprinkle his horse with dust, then rub some dust over his own hair and body. And after a battle, he must never take anything for himself.

All the while the horse and rider kept moving toward him. They seemed to be surrounded by a shadowy enemy. Arrows and bullets were streaking toward the long-haired rider but fell away without touching him. Then a crowd of people appeared, the rider's own people, it seemed, clutching at his arms, trying to hold him back, but he rode right through them, shaking them off. A fierce storm came up, but the man kept riding. A few hail spots appeared on his body, and a little zigzag streak of lightning on his cheek. The storm faded. A small red-backed hawk flew screaming over the man's head. Still the people grabbed at him, making a great noise, pressing close around him, grabbing, grabbing. But he kept riding.

The vision faded. Curly felt someone shaking him hard. When he looked up, he saw his father. Crazy Horse had ridden out into the prairie to search for the boy. He was angry that Curly had run off alone without saying a word, distracting everyone from the dying Conquering Bear.

When Curly told his father that he had gone out to fast for a vision, Crazy Horse was furious. Seeking a vision without instruction! Without purifying himself! Without any preparation at all! Curly decided not to say anything else, not then. He would tell his father about his vision, but he would wait for the right time.

A few days later, Conquering Bear died. That autumn, his relatives avenged his death. A party of Brulé warriors, led by Curly's uncle, Spotted Tail, rode down to the Platte River in war paint. They attacked a mail coach on the Holy Road, killing two drivers and a passenger.

The whites were clamoring for revenge, too. Eastern newspapers had reported that the "Grattan Massacre" was the result of a cunning Indian plot. The cow had been killed not for its meat and hide, the papers charged, but to lure the soldiers out of their fort.

An army investigator was sent to Fort Laramie. He reported that the Sioux had deliberately ambushed Lieutenant Grattan and his men. It was the first time that United States soldiers had been killed by Indians on the plains, and the army prepared to strike back.

5

"I Call Him Crazy Horse"

Like many other Sioux boys, Curly probably ran off to war before he reached his teens. A boy would hang around and eavesdrop as some warriors planned an expedition. He would watch enviously as they rode out of the village. That night he would slip quietly out of his tipi (his parents were sure to stop him if they awoke), grab his pony, and gallop off to catch up with the war party. The warriors would try to send him home, but after much pleading, he was usually allowed to tag along.

He became the war party's servant and errand boy, expected to fetch water, tend the horses, do whatever he was told. When fighting took place, he was ordered to stay behind and look after the traveling gear, so he had little chance to prove himself. Far from the scene of action, his chances of getting hurt were small, too.

But the war party did give him an opportunity to get the feel of an expedition, to learn the ways of war without actually fighting. From then on, he might join other war parties. And once he had been on an expedition, even as a water boy, he could smoke the pipe with the grown men.

Not every Sioux boy chose to be a warrior. A youngster might decide that

▶▶35◀◀

A war party's errand boy carrying a water bag.

he did not have the temperament or skills to be a good fighter. He might have a vision that would set him on a different life's course — becoming a holy man who listened and advised, like Curly's father, or a medicine man, learned in the art of healing, or in the conduct of rites and ceremonials. Depending on his special gifts, he might excel as a hunter, a horse catcher, or a band historian who recorded important events by painting pictures on animal skins. A boy could follow his own preference, but most Sioux boys wanted to earn a name for themselves as warriors. Eager for war honors, they waited impatiently for a chance to take part in a battle.

Curly's chance came during the summer of 1855, when he was about fourteen. While visiting his Brulé relatives, he went along on a horse-raiding expedition led by his uncle Spotted Tail to the country of the Pawnees and Omahas. Though he was supposed to be a helper rather than a fighting man, he found himself caught up in a battle with some Omahas. When he saw an enemy warrior creeping through the underbrush, he grabbed his bow and

Stealing horses from the lodges of the enemy.

fired an arrow. He knew he had made a good hit, because the Omaha straightened up, then fell forward.

Curly jumped from his horse and ran over, knife in hand, ready to take his first scalp. A scalp was a badge of honor, a sign of victory, and a symbol of the human spirit all in one. Like taking the feather of an eagle to share in the bird's power, taking the hair of a fighting man was a way to share the power of the defeated warrior who was willing to put his life on the line in battle.

Lifting his victim's hair, Curly was astonished to find that he had killed an Omaha woman. While this was not considered shameful during the heat of battle, he drew back. The girl who lay at his feet was as young and pretty as his own sister. Repulsed by what he had done, he turned away and let someone else take the scalp.

On the way home, leading some fine captured horses and carrying four Omaha scalps as war trophies, the warriors teased Curly for abandoning his. They made a little song about it, singing and laughing as they rode along:

A brave young man comes here
But a foolish one,
Without a good knife.

Later that summer, while Curly was still living with Spotted Tail and his Brulé relatives, runners arrived at their village with a warning from the government. Six hundred soldiers led by General William S. Harney were about to march through Brulé and Oglala territory, with orders to secure the Oregon Trail and strike terror into the hearts of any Sioux they met along the way. Messengers had gone out to all the Sioux bands in the region, telling them to move south of the Platte River or be considered hostile.

Most of the bands obeyed. But Spotted Tail's people saw no reason to move from their comfortable camp on Blue Water Creek, in the midst of the forbidden territory. They decided to wait until they could dry the meat and prepare the robes from a recent buffalo hunt. Little Thunder, the leading chief of Spotted Tail's band, considered himself a friend of the whites. Besides, the Brulés could not believe that anyone would dare attack a Sioux camp in Sioux territory.

Early in September, the Moon of Calves Growing Black Hair, Curly was out on the plains by himself, chasing a wild horse. Returning to the village late one afternoon, he picked up the scent of gunpowder, of burning skins and meat. When he reached the hills overlooking the Brulé camp, he saw smoke hanging over the ruined village. Below him, fires were smoldering. The bodies of dead warriors were strewn about, some of them blown to pieces by exploding cannonballs. He saw many dead women and children among the casualties, and some of the women had been scalped.

While Curly was away that morning, General Harney's cavalry troops had surrounded the village and launched a furious attack. The soldiers had killed eighty-six Indians and captured seventy women and children. The survivors had fled.

The sight of so many of his people dead in their own camp, of the destroyed tipis and possessions, all trampled and burned, filled Curly with a bitterness and rage that would haunt him for the rest of his life. The Sioux mourned even a single warrior's death. The loss of eight or ten warriors was considered a tribal calamity. No Sioux had ever witnessed what Curly saw before him now—the destruction of an entire Sioux village.

He heard moans and found a terrified young woman hiding in the bushes, her dead infant at her side. Her name was Yellow Woman. She was a Cheyenne who had been visiting relatives in the Brulé camp. Her husband and son had been killed during the fighting. Curly picked up an abandoned travois, tied it to his horse, and used it as a stretcher to carry Yellow Woman to safety. They followed the trail left by the fleeing Brulés until they caught up with them the next day. Many of the survivors were wounded, and almost everyone had lost relatives. Spotted Tail had fought bravely. Now he lay in his tipi, nursing the wounds from two pistol shots.

General Harney, meanwhile, had marched his captives in chains to Fort Laramie, a hundred miles to the west. There he demanded the surrender of the warriors who had attacked the mail coach on the Oregon Trail the year before.

Soon afterward, Spotted Tail and four of his comrades gave themselves up, so the women and children being held as hostages would be released. They rode into the fort dressed in their war finery and singing their death songs, for they expected to be hanged. Harney did, in fact, intend to hang them. But he was overruled by the Indian agent at Fort Laramie, the government official in charge of Indian affairs. Spotted Tail and his companions were sent to Fort Leavenworth, Kansas, where they were imprisoned for a year.

Harney was not yet finished with the Sioux. To show off his army's strength, he again marched through the heart of Sioux territory, looking for hostile bands, daring the Indians to come out and fight. None did. By now the Sioux had named Harney "Mad Bear," and they took care to keep out of his way.

When Harney reached Fort Pierre on the Missouri River, he summoned the chiefs from all the Teton Sioux tribes to a great council, held in the spring of 1856. There he dictated a new treaty, threatening to continue his military campaign and stop all trading unless the Sioux agreed once again to remain at peace and stay away from the emigrants on the Holy Road. Most of the chiefs signed the treaty. But unknown to Mad Bear Harney, the Sioux leaders quietly made plans among themselves to hold a council of their own the following year. They would meet at Bear Butte, an ancient Sioux gathering place just north of the Black Hills.

Curly traveled to Bear Butte with the Oglalas during the summer of 1857. Thousands of people had come to this sacred site, called together by tribal leaders who hoped that the Sioux could form a united front to resist the white men's invasion of their lands. Curly's whole family was there—his parents, his sister Laughing One, and his brother Little Hawk, who at the age of twelve already showed signs of becoming a daredevil warrior.

At Bear Butte, Curly had a chance to see some of the great heroes of the

Warriors carrying lances.

Teton Sioux nation, men he had heard about around winter campfires. Old Four Horns of the Hunkpapas from the north country was there with his young nephew, Sitting Bull. Lone Horn of the Miniconjous came to the council with his seven-foot-tall warrior son, Touch the Clouds. There were celebrated chiefs and warriors from the Sans Arcs, the Two Kettles, and the Blackfoot Sioux, and standing tall among them, prominent men from Curly's own Oglalas, respected leaders such as Old-Man-Afraid-of-His-Horses and rising younger warriors like the fiery Red Cloud of the Bad Face band. Only the Brulés stayed away. Spotted Tail and Little Thunder had had enough of fighting the whites.

As the Sioux leaders looked around them, at the vast camp circle that seemed as wide as the horizon, the strength of their people made their hearts strong again. Mad Bear's attack on Little Thunder's Brulé village had opened their eyes. Never in all their history had they suffered such losses in a single fight—nearly a hundred dead, women and children carried off as captives, a Sioux camp in the hands of the enemy.

The leaders met in a council lodge made of many painted hides laced together and stretched over special poles from the tall pines of the Black Hills. As they passed the sacred pipe of the Tetons, they agreed that they had given in too quickly to Mad Bear. They should have united and opposed him. They had already given up all of their country they could spare to the whites. Now they vowed to resist every white man who pushed in anywhere on Teton lands. They would stick together, for they were many.

Before leaving Bear Butte, Curly and his father spent some time by themselves. The boy was almost sixteen now, ready to accept his responsibilities as a warrior, and Crazy Horse wanted to talk to him. Together the father and son built a sweat lodge. They fasted and purified themselves in the scorching vapors of the lodge. It was then that Curly told his father about his vision, the dream that had come to him in the Nebraska Sand Hills while Conquering Bear was dying.

Crazy Horse listened with mounting excitement, for he believed that Curly had received a powerful medicine that would help him become a great leader of the Sioux. He told his son that the vision he had seen was of himself. He must be the rider on the horse. At all times he must do as that rider had done, dress like him, act like him. If he trusted his vision and followed the example of the rider, he could not be struck by enemy arrows or bullets. He must always be first in battle. And while his path might seem dark and dangerous, with opposition all around, and some of his people might try to hold him back, he must move fearlessly ahead. He must lead his people, and in battle he must never take anything for himself. Then his medicine, his sacred power, would not fail him.

The following summer, Curly was ready to prove himself in battle, eager to show that he could live up to the brave and selfless image that had appeared in his vision. He joined a horse-raiding expedition with his *kola,* Hump, another close friend named Lone Bear, his brother Little Hawk, and a few others. As buffalo had grown scarce around Fort Laramie and the Oregon Trail, the Oglalas had moved to the north and west. Curly and his companions now rode farther west than any Oglalas had traveled before. Their expedition took them all the way to the Wind River, land of the Shoshonis and Arapahos, a distant people who spoke a strange and unknown language.

When they discovered an Arapaho village with many fine horses, the Oglala warriors dressed themselves for battle. Each man put on his war paint and donned his sacred medicine objects in his own way. Curly prepared just as he had been instructed in his vision. He tied a small brown stone behind his ear, fastened a hawk's feather in his hair, and threw a handful of dust over his pony and himself. His only war paint was a little red lightning bolt on his cheek and a few hail spots on his body. Except for moccasins and a breechcloth, he rode naked into battle.

The Arapahos spotted the Oglalas and dug in on a hilltop behind some rocks. Curly and his comrades circled the enemy position again and again, whooping and hollering, clinging to their horses' flanks and shooting under their necks, but the Arapahos held them off.

Suddenly Curly charged forward by himself. In a spectacular show of

Counting coup.

daring, he galloped straight up the hill and right through the Arapaho stronghold, counting coup once, twice, three times—each time touching an enemy with his hand or bow, the greatest act of bravery a warrior could perform. Then he galloped away as arrows and bullets flew all around him, whizzing past his bare back, zinging off stones, spurting up gravel and dirt. His comrades at the foot of the hill called out his name to honor his bravery. His medicine in battle seemed very powerful indeed. Like the man in his vision, he rode safely through arrows and bullets without being hit.

As he reached his own men, he swung his pony around and charged again. This time two Arapahos rushed out to meet him. Curly killed one man with an arrow. He whirled around, fired again, and hit the second man. Then he leaped from his horse to take their scalps, but as he lifted the second scalp, an Arapaho arrow thumped into his leg. Just then his pony bolted. He had to run limping and stumbling down the hill, where he was pulled to safety by his comrades.

Hump cut the iron-tipped arrow from his friend's leg and wrapped the wound with a piece of fresh skin from a dead horse. In his excitement, Curly had forgotten the warning of his vision: *He should never take anything for himself.* Because he had taken the scalps, the power of his medicine had failed him. He vowed never to take another scalp.

When the Oglalas returned home, they were honored at a big victory dance. They had counted eight first coups, come away with some fine horses, and not lost a single man. One after another, the warriors stepped into the center of the circle that night and sang songs boasting of their brave deeds. And with each telling, the people sitting around the circle—the women and children and old men, the chiefs and warriors—shouted and cheered as the hero recited his exploits.

Curly was pushed forward into the circle twice. But each time he backed out silently, without saying a word, too shy to sing his own praises.

His father was not as modest. The next day, Crazy Horse celebrated his son's bravery. He put on his finest ceremonial blanket, the one with the beaded band across the middle, showing all the sacred things of his own holy vision. With this blanket over his shoulders, and his long braids fur-wrapped on his breast, Crazy Horse walked slowly around the village. He sang a song as he walked along, a song he had composed especially for this event:

> *My son has been against the people of an unknown tongue.*
> *He has done a brave thing.*
> *For this I give him a new name, the name of his father,*
> *and of many fathers before him —*
> *I give him a great name,*
> *I call him Crazy Horse.*

And so Crazy Horse the father gave away his name, passing it on to his brave warrior son. From then on the father called himself by a new name — Worm.

6

The Shirt-Wearer

For a few years after the big Teton Sioux council at Bear Butte, the Oglalas enjoyed some fat times. North of the Platte River, the plains still teemed with buffalo and other game. The whites were being caught up in their own Civil War, and for the moment, they paid little attention to the Indians on the northern plains.

The Oglalas had followed the buffalo herds far to the west of the Black Hills, to the headwaters of the Powder River. There they clashed time and again with their old enemies, the Crows and Shoshonis, fighting for possession of the rich Powder River hunting grounds. Oglala war parties went out each summer to raid the enemy tribes and give ambitious young warriors a chance to cover themselves with glory.

These raids rarely amounted to a full-scale battle. More often they were skirmishes that provided a stage for individual warriors to prove their courage. The object in an Indian fight was to win honors, not to kill enemies. The highest honors went to the man who counted coup by touching a live enemy with a bow, spear, or hand and getting away unharmed to boast about it.

Young Crazy Horse became a popular leader of expeditions against the

Chasing the Crows.

Crows and Shoshonis. Lean and lanky, an expert with the bow and a superb horseman, he performed many feats of bravery, fighting side by side with his friends Hump and Lone Bear and his brother Little Hawk. Other warriors admired his skill and cool courage. They were eager to join him so they could share in his powerful medicine.

He was also one of the best hunters among the Oglalas, bringing down many buffalo during tribal hunts. By himself he would ride out on the plains to hunt for deer, antelope, and elk, and for fat juicy ducks and geese during the spring and fall migrations. Often he stayed alone on the prairie for weeks at a time. When he returned from these solitary hunting trips, he gave most of the meat he brought back to widows and old folks.

People began to tell stories about his exploits, but even as his reputation grew, Crazy Horse remained unusually modest and reserved. He dressed plainly. He spent much of his time training his ponies and making bows and arrows. Sometimes he went to the lodge of his *akicita,* his warrior society, the Crow Owners, but he did not really enjoy the boisterous singing and rough jokes. He listened to his comrades boast about their brave deeds, while he himself said very little.

He was still living in his parents' lodge when he fell in love. Her name was Black Buffalo Woman. She was a niece of Red Cloud, a rising leader of the Bad Face band of the Oglalas. She had soft eyes, black hair that shimmered like moonbeams as it fell in braids down her back, and a laughing smile that attracted many young men.

Crazy Horse belonged to another band, the Hunkpatilas, but he had known Black Buffalo Woman since they were children. When he was nineteen or twenty, he began to court her seriously. On pleasant evenings he would ride over to the Bad Face camp and wait to meet Black Buffalo Woman at the door to her parents' lodge. There he would stand beside her in the traditional way, folding his courting blanket around the two of them so their heads were covered from view and they could enjoy a little talk, a little joking. For a few minutes he could smell the sweet-grass that perfumed her whitened deerskin dress and hear her shy, quick breathing inside the dark folds of the courting blanket.

But Black Buffalo Woman was very popular. Often, Crazy Horse had to

Wrapped in a courting blanket. Two other suitors are waiting their turn.

wait his turn as other suitors, courting blankets in hand, lined up outside her tipi. After exchanging a few words with one young man, she would laugh gaily, duck out from under his blanket, and move on to the next in line without looking back.

One of Crazy Horse's romantic rivals was a Bad Face warrior named No Water, a young follower of Red Cloud. In the summer of 1862, Red Cloud sent out word that he planned to lead a big war party against the Crows. Crazy Horse volunteered along with Hump, Lone Bear, and Little Hawk. No Water also joined the expedition with his brother Black Twin and several of their friends.

Shortly after the war party set out, No Water began to complain of a terrible toothache—a bad sign for a warrior whose medicine came from the two fierce grizzly bear teeth that he wore around his neck. Moaning and groaning, holding his face in his hand, No Water left the expedition and went home to his lodge.

Red Cloud's war party was gone for two weeks. When the warriors returned, Crazy Horse was pulled aside and told that No Water had married Black Buffalo Woman while they were away.

Some people whispered that Crazy Horse had been tricked. They said that Red Cloud had secretly arranged the marriage of his niece, because No Water belonged to an important and influential family. But Crazy Horse closed his ears to the rumors. Instead of joining the warriors' victory dance that night, he went directly to his parents' lodge and did not come out for several days.

Crazy Horse had never really known a white man until Caspar Collins came to visit his village. Collins was an army lieutenant stationed at Fort Laramie, where his father was in command. While many officers on the frontier looked upon the Indians as wild savages, Collins was truly interested in the life of the Sioux. He wanted to get to know the Sioux as people. In 1863, he traveled alone through Indian country, stopping off at various villages for a few days.

Crazy Horse took a liking to the young officer. The two men were about the same age, and they struck up an easy friendship. Crazy Horse invited Collins to his parents' lodge, helped him learn the Lakota dialect, showed him how to make a bow and arrows, and took him hunting for antelope and elk. They had some good laughs together as they compared the different customs of their two peoples.

While Collins was making friends with the Oglalas, trouble was brewing down south, in the valley of the Platte River. Wagon trains and stagecoaches crowded the Oregon Trail as more emigrants than ever before traveled west. Gold had been discovered in California back in 1849. Now another gold rush was taking place in Colorado. Thousands of fortune hunters were breaking off from the Oregon Trail and following new trails to mining camps in the Rocky Mountains.

The Colorado gold-rushers had driven one trail right through the heart of the Cheyennes' hunting grounds. Along the foothills of the Rockies, white ranchers and miners were settling in fertile valleys, taking over land that had been reserved for the Cheyennes by the Treaty of 1851.

"Almost all the Indians are just now liable to become hostile," reported Colonel William O. Collins, the Fort Laramie commander and the father of Caspar Collins. "The rush of emigrants through their country is immense, and their game is being rapidly destroyed or frightened away; the whites who come into contact with them generally know nothing about Indian habits or character and often do them injustice; and then [the Indians] complain that the treaty promises of the government are not kept."

As tensions mounted, violence flared again on the middle plains. Many of the regular army troops stationed on the frontier had been sent back east to fight in the Civil War. They had been replaced by volunteer militiamen. Often, these volunteers were rough-and-ready Indian haters who were spoiling for a fight. At the same time, tribal leaders in the region were finding it hard to keep their hot-blooded young warriors in check.

During the summer of 1864, fast-riding Indian war parties struck at wagon trains, ranches, and stagecoach stations, then disappeared onto the prairie. Armed bands of militiamen roamed the countryside, attacking unsuspecting villages and shooting at every Indian in sight. Many people on both sides were killed. Travel through the region stopped. All along the frontier, whites were thrown into a panic.

In September, several Cheyenne chiefs led by Black Kettle arranged a truce with Governor John Evans of Colorado Territory. They agreed to set up a peaceful camp at a little stream called Sand Creek, ninety miles southeast of Denver. Army officers pledged protection for the camp. Black Kettle raised both a large American flag and a white truce flag in front of his tipi to show that the village was friendly.

Despite this precaution, the village was attacked at dawn on November 29, 1864, in a surprise raid by six hundred Colorado militiamen. They were commanded by Colonel John M. Chivington, who had vowed to "punish" the Cheyennes by killing as many of them as possible, "big and little." When a junior officer protested that the Cheyennes were at peace, Chivington roared back, "Damn any man who sympathizes with Indians! I have come to kill Indians and believe it is right and honorable to use any means under God's heaven to kill Indians!"

When the fighting ended that morning, 105 Cheyenne women and children and 28 men had been shot down. Chivington had nine men killed and thirty-eight wounded, many of them victims of careless firing by the soldiers against one another. Afterward, the militiamen scalped and mutilated the dead Indians, plundered their tipis, and divided up the Cheyennes' horse herd. Among the dead was Yellow Woman, the Cheyenne who had been rescued by Crazy Horse nine years earlier after the army's attack on Little Thunder's village.

The survivors fled south on foot and found refuge with other Cheyennes. Black Kettle still argued for peace, but his words were no longer heard by the furious warriors who had seen their wives, mothers, and children slaughtered by white militiamen. Word of the attack spread like a prairie fire as runners carried war pipes to Indians all across the central plains—to their fellow Cheyennes, and to their allies among the Oglalas, the Brulés, and the Arapahos. The Sand Creek Massacre, as it was now called, set off a bloody war of revenge.

That winter, Indian war parties created havoc all along the South Platte River. Crazy Horse rode south with his friends to join the big allied Indian encampment in the valley of the South Platte. He was one of the warriors who raided the stagecoach station at Julesburg, Colorado. They plundered the station's store and warehouse, burned the buildings to the ground, then rode away.

The raids continued throughout January 1865, the Moon of Frost on the

Galloping warriors.

Lodge. For a hundred miles along the South Platte, warriors burned stage stations and ranches, drove off horses and cattle, and destroyed telegraph lines, killing more people than Chivington had killed at Sand Creek. The Indians controlled the South Platte valley so completely, they kept huge bonfires burning at night to guide the returning war parties. Finally, led by northern Sioux, the entire allied Indian force pulled back to the wilderness of the Powder River country, where there were no soldiers or forts.

Army reinforcements were rushed to the plains. At Fort Laramie, plans were made for the U.S. Army to invade the Powder River country and overpower the hostile tribes. About two thousand Sioux, the "Laramie Loafers," were living in tipi villages around the fort. They were regarded as friendlies, but to avoid trouble, army officers decided to move them out of the region. In July, the Moon of Cherries Ripening, the army began to march the Loafer Indians under military guard down the Platte River to Fort Kearney, Nebraska, about three hundred miles to the east.

When the unarmed Indians realized with alarm that they were being taken into the territory of their dreaded enemies, the Pawnees, they sent runners to their Powder River relatives, begging for help. Crazy Horse was part of a war party that rode south and attacked the marching column at Horse Creek, driving the soldiers into a corral and pinning them down until the Loafers escaped. Most of the Indians fled to Sioux camps in the north.

Later that month, the Indians showed their strength again when they raided the army garrison at the Platte Bridge stage station on the North Platte River. This was a massive expedition, the biggest war party anyone could remember. Some three thousand warriors from several tribes took part. Among the leaders were Red Cloud of the Oglala Sioux and Roman Nose of the Northern Cheyennes.

Crazy Horse had been a member of several successful war parties that year. Now he was chosen by the war chiefs as one of twenty decoys who would try to lure the soldiers at the Platte Bridge garrison into an ambush.

At daybreak on July 25, 1865, the decoys were ready. Crazy Horse threw a handful of dust over his pony and himself. With a hawk's feather in his hair, a red lightning streak painted on his cheek, and his medicine stone behind his ear, he trotted off with the other decoys, riding down a hillside toward the wooden bridge that crossed the North Platte. At the opposite end of the bridge stood the military post—a stockade, stage station, and telegraph office.

As the decoys approached the bridge, they began to shake out their buffalo robes and shout, as though they were trying to stampede the army horses grazing across the river. But the plan failed. Soldiers galloped out of the fort and chased the decoys only a short distance before warriors concealed in the hills burst impatiently out of their hiding places. The soldiers took one look, saw hundreds of Indians appearing on the hilltops, and beat a hasty retreat back to their stockade.

The next day the decoys tried every trick they knew to lure the soldiers out of their fort again. They were about to give up when they saw a troop of cavalrymen gallop out of the stockade and across the river, their horses' hooves clattering on the bridge. They were not crossing to attack the decoys, however, but to warn an unsuspecting train of military freight wagons that was coming up the trail.

Here was the chance the Indians had been waiting for. Cascading down from the hills, several hundred warriors overwhelmed both the cavalry troopers and the oncoming wagon train, killing many of the whites and plundering the wagons before withdrawing to their camp in the hills.

"As we went into the troops," one of the warriors recalled, "I saw an officer on a bay horse rush past me through the dense clouds of dust and smoke. His horse was running away from him . . . the lieutenant had an arrow sticking in his forehead and his face was streaming with blood." Crazy Horse learned later that the fatally wounded officer was his old friend, Lieutenant Caspar Collins.

That year, Crazy Horse received the highest honor his people could give a young warrior. The Oglalas had seven tribal elders, men over forty who were known as the "Big Bellies." Chosen by common consent, they were recognized as the tribe's leaders. After returning from the fight at Platte Bridge, the Big Bellies met in a council lodge painted with sacred designs. Sitting in the middle of the seven elders, a place of honor, was Old-Man-Afraid-of-His-Horses. Together they selected four outstanding young warriors to act as their assistants, to be "shirt-wearers," or protectors of the people.

When the elders had made their choices, the chiefs of the *akicitas*, the warrior societies, rode around the village four times. Each time they called out the name of one of the young men who had been chosen. The first three—Young-Man-Afraid-of-His-Horses, Sword, and American Horse—were the sons of Big Bellies, members of important families. The fourth time the war chiefs rode around the village, they called out the name of Crazy Horse, the son of a humble holy man.

Crazy Horse was led to the council lodge, which now had its sides rolled up so that all could see and hear what was done there. The newly selected shirt-wearers were seated on buffalo robes in the middle of the lodge, facing the seven Big Bellies. All around them, filling up the lodge and spilling out beyond its rolled-up sides, were other young warriors with their fathers, and behind them, the women and children.

After a feast of roasted buffalo and boiled dog, the chosen warriors were presented with fine new sheepskin shirts dyed with blue and yellow or red and green pigments. Across the shoulders and along the arms of the shirts were bands of quillwork with pictures of men and weapons. The sleeves were fringed with locks of hair. Each lock represented a brave deed—a horse captured, a wound received, a prisoner taken or a scalp, a coup counted, a friend's life saved, or some other great thing done. Crazy Horse had 240 locks on his shirt.

An elderly man respected for his wisdom rose to instruct the shirt-wearers on their duties. They would lead the warriors in camp and on the march, making sure that order was preserved and that the rights of every Oglala man, woman, and child were respected. They must look out especially for the poor, the widows, and the orphans—all those of little power. It would be hard at times to discharge their responsibilities, the old man told them, but they had been chosen because they were bighearted, generous, brave, and strong.

Crazy Horse was the youngest of the newly appointed shirt-wearers. At twenty-four, he had become a leader of his people.

7

Red Cloud's War

After the big fight at Platte Bridge, two thousand soldiers marched north from Fort Laramie. Their commander, General Patrick E. Connor, planned to seek out and destroy the Indians' Powder River camps. "You will receive no overtures of peace or submission from the Indians," Connor told his troops, "but will attack and kill every male Indian over twelve years old."

The army intended to teach the wild Sioux and Cheyennes a lesson. And while they were at it, Connor's soldiers would help make the Powder River country safe for white travelers.

Gold had now been discovered in the mountains of Montana. The shortest route to the newly opened mines was a trail pioneered by John Bozeman, which cut straight through the Sioux's Powder River hunting grounds. Bozeman's trail branched off from the Oregon Trail at Fort Laramie and led north to the booming mining camps around Virginia City, Montana. But the Indians stood in the way. Few white men were willing to risk traveling on the Bozeman Trail without military protection.

General Connor's Powder River campaign turned out to be a disaster. Crazy Horse and his fellow warriors were watching from a distance as Connor's soldiers wandered through the unmapped countryside, searching for Indian villages to attack. War parties would appear out of nowhere. The Indians attacked the soldiers' flanks, raided their camps, and ran off their horses. Within a few weeks, the troops were slaughtering their remaining horses for food. Finally they retreated back to the safety of Fort Laramie, ragged, hungry, and footsore.

By then, a public outcry over the brutal massacre at Sand Creek had forced the army to soften its policy toward the Indians. If only the Indians were treated fairly, peace advocates argued, a just settlement could be worked out that would meet the needs of both sides.

Government commissioners traveled to the frontier with a new treaty of peace and friendship. Once again, they promised plenty of gifts and yearly annuities, including guns and ammunition for hunting, for those who agreed to sign. In return, the whites wanted the right to use the Bozeman Trail and build forts to protect it.

The peace commissioners persuaded a few friendly chiefs to put their marks on the new treaty and collect their gifts. But other Sioux leaders, representing thousands of people living in the Black Hills and the Powder River country, refused to meet with the commissioners. Except for a few traders, they wanted all whites to get out of their country and quit traveling through it. They knew that other hunting grounds had been ruined when the whites built roads through them.

At last, in June 1866, the Moon of Making Fat, Red Cloud, Old Man Afraid, Spotted Tail, and other leading chiefs of the Oglalas and Brulés decided it would do no harm to visit Fort Laramie and see for themselves what the white men had to say. Crazy Horse and many of the younger warriors did not want them to go. They argued that the Sioux were living well in

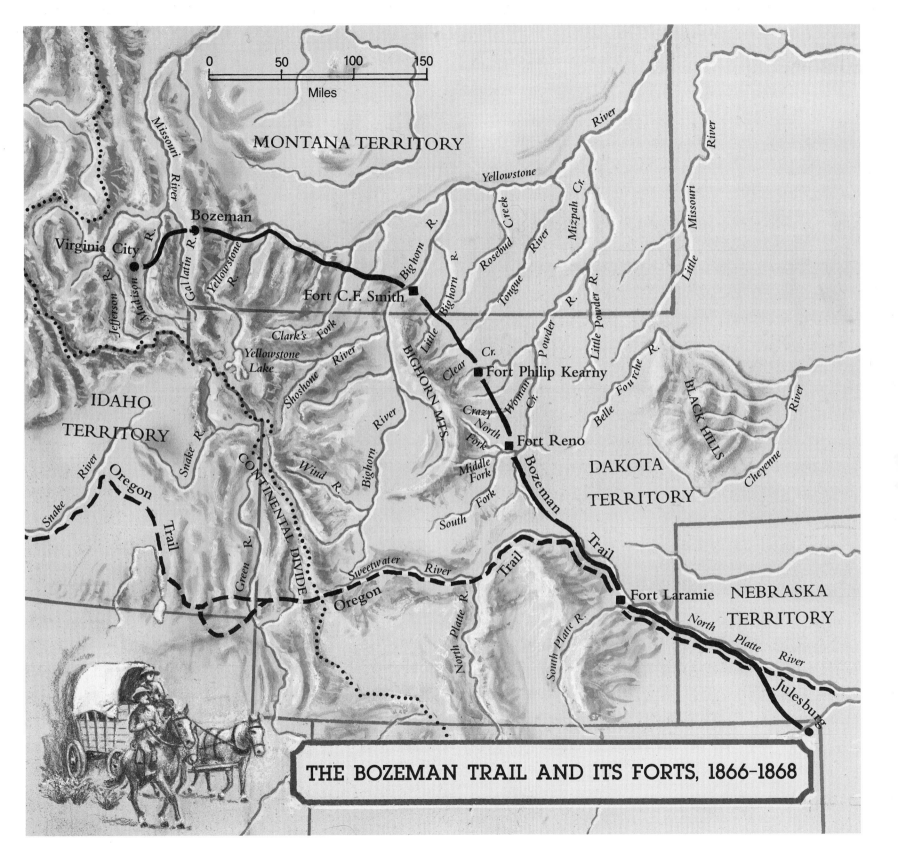

THE BOZEMAN TRAIL AND ITS FORTS, 1866–1868

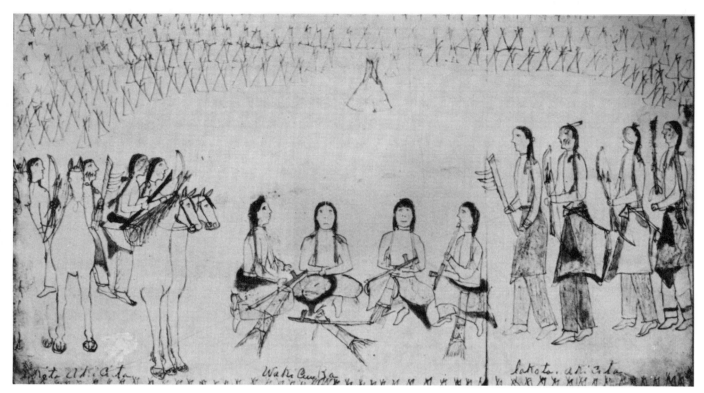

A meeting of four village councilmen. Members of a warrior's society, an akicita, *wait to receive their orders.*

the Powder River country and had no need of the white men or their presents. But Red Cloud and the others were willing to talk. They rode down to Fort Laramie and asked to have the new treaty explained to them.

The commissioners tried to reassure the chiefs. They promised that white travelers on the Bozeman Trail would not disturb the Indians' hunting grounds or disrupt their way of life. Simply by touching the pen and agreeing to the treaty, the Sioux could get the guns and ammunition that were always in such short supply among them.

As the two sides negotiated, an infantry regiment commanded by Colonel Henry B. Carrington marched into Fort Laramie. Carrington caused an uproar at the peace council when he revealed that he had been ordered to build forts on the Bozeman Trail regardless of the council's outcome. The angry chiefs accused the commissioners of deceiving them. None of them had been told anything about the army's plan.

Red Cloud charged that the commissioners had treated the chiefs like children. They had only been pretending to negotiate, while planning all along to take the Powder River country by force.

"The white men have crowded the Indians back year by year, until we are forced to live in a small country north of the Platte," Red Cloud declared, his black eyes blazing with anger. "Now our last hunting ground is to be taken from us. Our women and children will starve, but for my part, I prefer to die by fighting rather than starvation.

"I will talk with you no more! I will go—now!—and I will fight you! As

A war party on horseback.

long as I live, I will fight you for the last hunting grounds of my people!"

Red Cloud stormed out of the meeting, followed by most of his fellow chiefs. The next day they headed back to the Powder River. Spotted Tail was one of those who stayed behind. He had been the first to take to the warpath after the killing of Conquering Bear twelve years before, but now he was an advocate of peace. During his imprisonment at Fort Leavenworth, he became deeply impressed with the power of the United States. He was convinced that his people must follow a path of peace and accommodation if they were to survive.

Carrington and his soldiers marched north. That summer they built three forts on the Bozeman Trail as Sioux warriors watched from the hills. While the forts were going up, Red Cloud was riding across the northern plains, carrying a war pipe to all the Sioux tribes in the region, and to the Northern Cheyennes and Arapahos. He invited them to join in an all-out offensive against the whites, a war to save their hunting grounds and the herds of buffalo on which they lived.

By the time Carrington's forts were ready, Red Cloud had recruited a force of two thousand fighting men. At the age of forty-five, he was one of the most admired war leaders among the Sioux. He would provide the overall leadership of the campaign against the whites. Crazy Horse, now in his mid-twenties and newly appointed as a shirt-wearer, would serve as one of Red Cloud's chief lieutenants. In the months to come, he would lead dozens of war parties ranging as far south as Fort Laramie.

Carrington announced that travelers could now use the Bozeman Trail in safety. But as soon as the first travelers set out, Crazy Horse and his comrades launched a hit-and-run guerrilla war—raiding all along the trail, striking at wagon trains and military convoys, running off horses and cattle from the forts themselves, attacking anyone who dared venture outside the stockades. Crazy Horse went out on war parties almost every day, usually with Hump, Lone Bear, his brother Little Hawk, and Young Man Afraid.

During the first five months of fighting, between August and December 1866, Indians killed 154 soldiers and travelers and captured hundreds of horses, cattle, and mules. All traffic on the "Bloody Bozeman" came to a halt. Carrington's forts were isolated and in a state of siege.

Much of the fighting centered around Fort Phil Kearny, which had been built on a grassy plateau, so that Indians could not approach unseen. The nearest stand of trees was about five miles to the west, along the slopes of the Bighorn Mountains. Woodcutters went out regularly with a military escort to chop trees for the fort's cooking, heating, and construction needs. Using captured binoculars, Red Cloud could observe this activity from the ridges overlooking the fort. With blanket wavings and mirror signals, he could direct Crazy Horse and the other warriors who attacked at every opportunity before vanishing into the countryside.

The soldiers were armed with single-shot rifles, while only a few of the Indians had guns. Red Cloud felt that he could win a decisive victory if he could lure a large force of soldiers away from the fort, where the Indians could overwhelm them by sheer numbers, using arrows, spears, and clubs. He began to plan an ambush.

The first two attempts at an ambush failed when excitable young warriors revealed their positions and sent the soldiers retreating back to the fort. Late in December, the Moon of Popping Trees, Red Cloud and his fellow war leaders prepared to try again. This time, every detail of the Indians' plan was plotted carefully in advance. Red Cloud had picked Crazy Horse as one of the decoys who would lure the soldiers into a trap. Like actors preparing for a play, the decoys rehearsed every movement they would make.

On the evening of December 20, Red Cloud and the other war leaders gathered to consult a *winkte,* a man who dressed and lived as a woman. *Wink-tes* enjoyed a special place in Sioux society because they were thought to have unusual powers, including the ability to predict the future. Pulling a black cloth over his head, the *winkte* rode over the hills, seeking a vision. When he returned, he cried out: "I have ten men, five in each hand. Do you want them?" The leaders shook their heads and told him that he had not brought them enough enemies.

Three more times the *winkte* rode off, zigzagging his pony and tooting on a bone whistle. Each time he returned with a larger number of enemies in his hands. After his fourth trip, he came galloping back, greatly excited. Swaying back and forth, he fell off his pony, struck the ground with both fists, and gasped, "My hands are full. I have a hundred or more!" The war leaders gave a great shout of approval and returned to their camp.

The next morning a logging detail left Fort Kearny to collect firewood along Big Piney Creek. The day was bright and cold, with patches of snow covering the hillsides. As the woodcutters headed toward the creek, a small party of Indians swept down from the hills. The loggers quickly made a defensive corral with their wagons and signaled the fort for aid.

Inside the fort, bugles sounded. A relief force of cavalry troops and infantrymen was organized and placed under the command of Captain William J. Fetterman, a young officer who had been itching for a real fight with the Sioux. Fetterman had often expressed contempt for the Indians' fighting abilities. "Give me eighty men," he had boasted, "and I'll ride through the entire Sioux nation." As it happened, when he rode out of the fort that morning to rescue the loggers, he was in command of exactly eighty men.

Fetterman and his troops were advancing toward the loggers when the Indians suddenly called off their attack and began to withdraw. Just then, a few other Indians popped up near the walls of the fort. They were moving slowly along the edge of the brush, some on horseback, some on foot, trying to stay out of sight. Two howitzer shells fired from the fort exploded over their heads, knocking one warrior off his horse. The others howled and yelled. Zigzagging back and forth, they scattered.

All of this happened in a matter of minutes. Fetterman paused. He looked around, trying to decide what to do. In the distance, the Indians who had attacked the loggers were already disappearing into the hills. Closer to him, the warriors who had been hiding in the brush near the fort were still within striking distance. For once he had caught a small group of Indians out in the open.

Those warriors were Red Cloud's handpicked decoys. There were ten of them—two Cheyennes, two Arapahos, and six Sioux: Crazy Horse, his friends Hump and Lone Bear, and the Sioux shirt-wearers He Dog, Young Man Afraid, and American Horse. Crazy Horse had been given the honor of leading them. It was so cold that morning that he had not stripped for battle as he usually did, but had kept his blanket belted around him. As usual, he had a red lightning streak on his cheek, hail spots on his body, a hawk's feather pinned to his hair, and his medicine stone behind his ear.

Crazy Horse knew exactly how to catch Fetterman's attention. He charged toward the soldiers on his horse, whooping and waving his blanket, then dashed off, as though he were trying to hold the soldiers off while his fellow warriors got away. Fetterman took the bait. He signaled his troops to give chase.

The decoys had rehearsed their role well. Fetterman's troops were part cavalry, part infantrymen on foot, so the captain advanced slowly enough to keep his men together. The decoys moved back just as slowly, taunting the soldiers, shouting threats and insults, staying just beyond the range of the soldiers' rifles.

Once, Crazy Horse jumped off his horse as though something was wrong.

He lifted the animal's foot, shook his head, and began to lead the horse by the bridle, running alongside. The other decoys closed around him, as if to protect him. As Fetterman and his troops drew closer, bullets began to zing over the decoys' heads and kick up puffs of snow and dirt all around them. At the last minute, Crazy Horse leaped back on his horse, and with the other decoys, headed toward Lodge Pole Ridge, leading the soldiers on.

Fetterman had been ordered not to chase the Indians beyond the ridge, but there were only ten Indians armed with bows and arrows against his eighty well-armed men. And he had almost caught them! Shouting to his men to hurry, the captain chased the decoys over the top of the ridge and down into Peno Valley beyond. The fort was now out of sight.

Hiding in the hills on either side of Peno Creek were two thousand Cheyennes, Arapahos, and Sioux. They waited. Suddenly the decoys split into two groups, then veered and rode quickly across each other's trail. That was the signal. The warriors sprang from their hiding places in high grass and behind rocks and came screaming down the hillsides, charging into the troops from every direction, showering them with arrows, swinging their hatchets and war clubs. The soldiers tried to defend themselves with their rifles and bayonets, but they were quickly overwhelmed as the Indians clubbed them to the ground.

When the last shot was fired, Fetterman and every one of his eighty men lay dead on the battlefield. The Indians said later that thirteen warriors had been killed, several of them shot by Indian arrows during the chaos of battle. Crazy Horse's close friend Lone Bear was among the casualties. Crazy Horse and Hump searched for him after the fight and found him lying among some rocks, barely alive. He was so badly wounded that he could not crawl away. He had survived only long enough to die in Crazy Horse's arms.

The warriors moved swiftly among the dead, stripping the soldiers of their clothing, their weapons, and their scalps. One soldier who had displayed exceptional courage, Private Adolf Metzger, however, was not touched. A burial detail later found his body fully dressed, unscalped, and covered with a buffalo robe.

It was the worst defeat the United States Army had ever suffered in Indian warfare. The Indians called it the Battle of the Hundred Slain. To the

Warriors attacking cavalrymen.

stunned and disbelieving whites, it became known as the Fetterman Massacre.

For months afterward, Red Cloud's force of Sioux, Cheyennes, and Arapahos kept up the pressure. The three forts on the Bozeman Trail were in a constant state of siege. Soldiers manning the forts had to fight just to get food and water. Gradually it became clear that the government had to make peace or face a long and bloody conflict.

Once again, a peace commission traveled to Fort Laramie. This time the commissioners brought a new treaty that appeared to meet the Indians' demands. All of present-day South Dakota west of the Missouri River would be set aside by the government as the "Great Sioux Reservation," a region that the Sioux could keep forever. The government would establish agencies on the reservation, issue clothing and food, build schools, and teach the Indians to support themselves by farming. Hopefully, they would exchange their bows and arrows for shovels and plows.

The Powder River country—the vast region to the west of the reservation—would be declared "unceded Indian territory." No whites would be allowed to enter that region. Those Sioux who wished to live by the chase could remain in the Powder River country, which was guaranteed as an Indian sanctuary as long as the buffalo lasted. As usual, plenty of gifts were promised to every chief who agreed to sign the new treaty.

Aside from making peace, the commissioners had another goal in mind. The new reservation would keep the Sioux safely away from the nation's first transcontinental railroad, the Union Pacific, which followed the route of the Oregon Trail as it advanced across the plains. All over the Great Plains, Indian tribes were being coaxed or forced onto reservations, where they could be watched and controlled.

In the spring of 1868, a number of Sioux chiefs were persuaded to visit

Fort Laramie and agree to this new treaty. Red Cloud—backed by Crazy Horse and the other shirt-wearers—continued to hold out. He insisted that the Bozeman Trail forts be abandoned before any treaty could be signed, because he had no faith in the white men's word. He sent a message to the commissioners: "We are in the mountains looking down at the soldiers and the forts. When we see the soldiers moving away and the forts abandoned, then I will come down and talk."

Finally the government gave in to Red Cloud's demands. That summer the three Bozeman Trail forts were evacuated and the trail was abandoned. As soon as the soldiers had packed their gear and marched away, Crazy Horse led his torch-bearing warriors down from the hills and they burned the forts to ashes.

Red Cloud waited a little longer. Then, after a special Oglala council had granted its approval, he traveled to Fort Laramie, where he joined 125 other Sioux leaders on November 6, 1868. After putting his name to the treaty, he rose to make a speech. He was ready for peace, he said. It would be difficult for him to control the young warriors, but as for himself, he intended to live up to the treaty's terms. Meanwhile, he planned to return to the Powder River, where he would continue to live by the chase. The Sioux did not know how to farm, he said. And as long their country was filled with buffalo, they did not care to learn.

8

Treaty Troubles

Crazy Horse had every right to rejoice. He had helped drive the Crows and Shoshonis from the Powder River country, pushing those tribes back to the Bighorn Mountains. And he had played a leading role in closing down the army's forts and chasing the soldiers from the Bozeman Trail. Free of the whites at last, he could live as he pleased in what was now his people's home territory—spectacular land teeming with buffalo and other wild game.

In his late twenties, he still looked boyish with his slender build and narrow face framed by long, fur-wrapped braids. When combed out, his brown hair hung down his back almost to his waist. People praised his courage and skill as a warrior and hunter, but above all, they admired his generosity. He would return from his solitary hunting trips with gifts of fresh meat for the old folks, for widows and orphans. Anyone in need could count on a helping hand from Crazy Horse.

As a war leader, he was forceful and inspiring. But at home in his village, he remained a quiet loner who spent much time by himself. Though a shirt-wearer, he seldom attended leadership councils. And when he did attend, he rarely spoke. "In his own tipi he would joke, and when he was on the warpath with a small party, he would joke to make his warriors feel good," remembered Black Elk, a younger cousin of Crazy Horse. "But around the village he hardly noticed anybody, except little children."

Children seemed to bring out the storyteller in Crazy Horse. They would gather around and sit at his feet as he told the Sioux hero tales that he had heard himself as a child. He also enjoyed coaching the boys of the village, teaching them tricks he had learned as a hunter and warrior—how to snare and track small animals, how to make a stronger bow, how to calm a skittish pony.

Unmarried, he continued to live with his parents in their lodge. People whispered that he was still in love with Black Buffalo Woman. He had never stopped yearning for her, they said. By now she had three children by No Water, the youngest an infant in a cradleboard. Crazy Horse was often seen visiting her village. He would watch from a distance as she carried water

Indian love flute.

from the stream or played with her children. Now and then they exchanged a few words. And when Crazy Horse left to return home, people noticed Black Buffalo Woman looking after him as he rode away, sitting tall on his pony, his long brown braids swinging at his sides.

The friendly feelings that had followed the signing of the Fort Laramie Treaty did not last long. Before a year had passed, the Indians and the government were arguing bitterly over the terms of the treaty, which meant one thing to the chiefs who had signed it and another to the whites.

Because of the fighting on the Bozeman Trail, the Powder River Sioux had not been able to visit a trading post for nearly five years. Their camps were overflowing with buffalo robes that they wanted to barter for guns and other trade goods. Now that the fighting had ended and the treaty was signed, they expected to start trading freely again.

That's not what happened. When a band of Oglalas traveled south to trade at Platte Bridge Station, soldiers warned them off and then fired on them, wounding a chief. The government had banned all trade along the Platte. The army had been ordered to keep roving Indian bands away from the river—and away from the Oregon Trail and the Union Pacific Railroad.

Red Cloud and his fellow chiefs were furious when they heard about this. They accused the government of bad faith. They had been lied to and deceived, they said.

The government claimed that the Sioux were violating the terms of the Fort Laramie Treaty, going back on their word. They must settle on the Great Sioux Reservation, where they could trade at government agencies, or else stay in the wild Powder River country and do without trade goods.

The Sioux complained that the treaty's complicated wording about taking up farming and sending their children to the white men's schools had never been properly explained to them. Red Cloud declared again that his people did not wish to be farmers. With a spacious reservation to live on, if they wished, and unlimited hunting rights in the Powder River country to the west, he still believed that the Sioux could control their own destiny.

Most of the younger war leaders like Crazy Horse weren't even thinking about moving to the reservation. They had fought to save the only hunting grounds left to them. That's where they meant to stay, pitching their camps in the valleys of the clear rivers, hunting buffalo in the shadow of the Bighorn Mountains. Crazy Horse was happy to be living the free life he loved best, happy to be as free as the wind that bends the buffalo grass. With his fellow warriors, he felt strong and confident in the Powder River country. He was certain that the Sioux could meet any future threat from the army.

General William Tecumseh Sherman, commander of the United States Army, had other ideas. He regarded the Fort Laramie Treaty of 1868 as a temporary truce rather than a permanent peace settlement. Sherman was convinced that sooner or later all Indians would have to be driven onto reservations. With that in mind, he encouraged the slaughter of the remaining buffalo herds. As the nation's new railroads pushed westward across the plains, white hunters would exterminate the buffalo, forcing the Indians to give up the hunt and become wards of the government. Let the Sioux chase the buffalo and fight the Crows for a few more years, Sherman said. When the time came, they would have to move to the reservation. They would have no other choice.

In 1870, the government persuaded Red Cloud, Spotted Tail, and a large delegation of other Sioux leaders to travel to Washington, D.C., where they would meet President Ulysses S. Grant and discuss their complaints. During the trip, officials made sure that the Indians saw for themselves the enormous power of the United States. The chiefs toured Washington in carriages, witnessed the sights and wonders of the great city, and visited the Senate while it was in session. At the U.S. Arsenal, they saw more guns in a single building than they had ever seen in their entire lives.

One weapon was a huge new cannon with a barrel almost wide enough for a man to crawl into. Red Cloud watched silently as the gun was fired. The shell went screaming over the Potomac River and could be seen skipping across the water four or five miles away.

Red Cloud insisted that he had come to Washington for one reason only: to secure the right of the Indians to trade peaceably along the Platte River. When the full text of the 1868 treaty was finally read to him and his fellow chiefs, so much in it seemed new to them that the Indians protested again. They had not been told truthfully what the sixteen articles of the treaty really said, they claimed. Now, for the first time, they were hearing all the false things that were in it. "I signed a treaty of peace," Red Cloud shouted, "but it was not this one! This one is all lies!"

The Sioux leaders traveled on to New York, where Red Cloud delivered an eloquent speech in defense of his people, charging the whites with a long list of betrayals and deceptions. His appearance before a large and sympathetic crowd at Cooper Union caused such a sensation, the government agreed to a compromise. Red Cloud went home with permission to trade at Fort Laramie.

Even so, he was a changed man. His glimpses of the white men's world had convinced him that armed resistance was futile. He had been impressed by the vast riches and power of the whites. He knew that the buffalo were vanishing, and with their passing the Sioux would have to change their way of life.

In 1871, the government established a special reservation agency for Red

Cloud's Oglalas on the North Platte River, about thirty miles east of Fort Laramie. Another agency was built on the White River north of the Platte for Spotted Tail's Brulés. Red Cloud put away his warrior's clothing. From then on, he worked to protect his people's interests as a politician rather than a warrior. He never again lived in the Powder River country he had fought so hard to defend.

Now all the Sioux were faced with a tough choice. They could give up the hunt, settle on the reservation, and yield their independence to white offi-

Riding home with meat.

cials. Or they could reject any contact with the whites and hold to the old ways, as far away from the whites as possible.

When Red Cloud moved to the reservation, Crazy Horse and many other Oglalas refused to follow him. They had not closed the Bozeman Trail and burned the soldiers' forts simply to become reservation Indians, they said. They had fought to remain free, living as they wished by hunting the buffalo. They did not trust the whites and did not want to move near them for any reason.

In fact, some of the Oglalas, including Crazy Horse, were now suspicious of Red Cloud. They felt that he had given up the fight for freedom and sold out to the white men. And there were others who felt the same way, influential leaders like Sitting Bull of the Hunkpapa Sioux, Two Moons of the Northern Cheyennes, and Spotted Eagle of the Sans Arcs. These men had never recognized the Fort Laramie Treaty. They had agreed to nothing. They were content to stay outside the boundaries of the Sioux reservation. Red Cloud had lost their respect. "The white people have put bad medicine over Red Cloud's eyes," said Sitting Bull, "to make him see everything and anything they please."

With Red Cloud gone to the reservation, the Powder River Oglalas looked for new leadership to warriors like Crazy Horse and Hump. Crazy Horse wanted nothing more than to be left alone by the whites, and he was held in high regard by those who shared his feelings.

9

Crazy Horse Elopes

At about this time, the Crow Owners' Society presented a new honor to Crazy Horse and his comrade He Dog. The two warriors were named lance bearers. It was their duty to carry the ancient lances of the Oglalas into battle. "These spears were each three or four hundred years old," He Dog remembered, "and were given by the older generation to those in the younger generation who had best lived the life of a warrior."

When a war party set out to raid the Crows one summer, Crazy Horse and He Dog rode at the head of the column, holding the sacred lances high as the scalps and feathers tied to them fluttered in the wind. Oglala scouts found a big Crow camp between the Bighorn and Little Bighorn rivers, on land that was part of the Crows' new reservation. Crazy Horse and He Dog led the attack, carrying the lances throughout the fighting. They were always the first to charge and the last to retreat when the Crows counterattacked.

The Oglalas chased the Crows all the way back to their reservation agency, where the enemy warriors pitched camp under the protection of the U.S. soldiers' guns. The Oglalas camped a short distance away. For several days they taunted the Crows, raided their horse herd, and dared them to fight

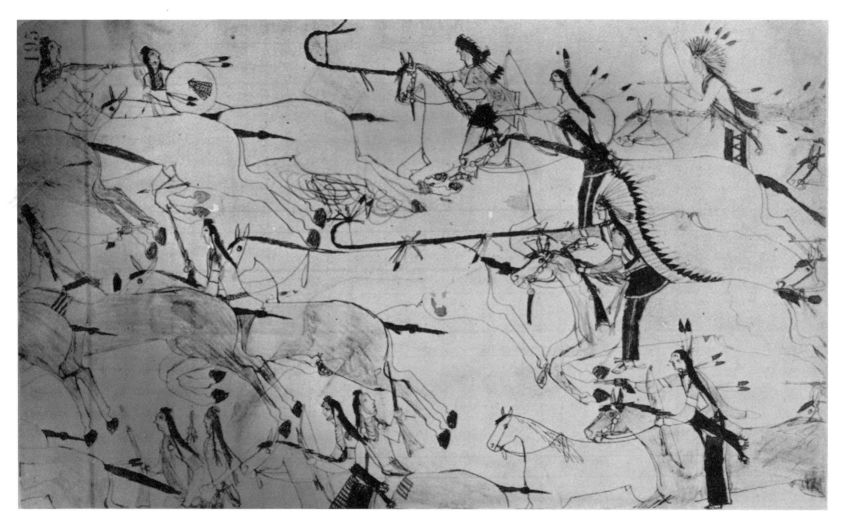

A battle with the Crows.

back. When the Sioux finally returned to the Powder River, they held a big victory dance. From then on, the Oglalas called that fight "When They Chased the Crows Back to Camp."

But there were other expeditions that did not turn out as well. Late one autumn, when Crazy Horse, He Dog, and Hump led a war party against the Shoshonis, they found themselves riding through a drizzly rain that was turning to snow. Their horses sloshed through mud and slush, sinking in over their ankles. Crazy Horse wanted to call off the expedition, but Hump wouldn't hear of it. Not long before, they had called off another fight in the same place.

Years later, He Dog recalled the conversation that day:

"The last time you called off a fight here, when we got back to camp they laughed at us," Hump told Crazy Horse. "You and I have our good names to think about. If you don't care about it, you can go back. But I'm going to stay here and fight."

"All right, we'll fight, if you feel that way about it," Crazy Horse replied. "But I think we're going to get a good licking. You have a good gun and I have a good gun, but look at our men! None of them have good guns, and most of them have only bows and arrows. It's a bad place for a fight and a bad day for it, and the enemy are twelve to our one."

They stayed to fight, but as Crazy Horse had predicted, the Shoshonis proved too strong for them. Soon the Oglalas were on the run, with Crazy Horse, Hump, and Good Weasel acting as a rearguard. Then Hump's horse was hit in the leg and began to stumble in the mud. As the Shoshonis pressed closer, Crazy Horse and Good Weasel tried to hold them back, but Hump's horse went down and enemy warriors surged over him.

On that cold autumn day, Crazy Horse lost his oldest friend, his beloved *kola* who had shared his boyhood and fought by his side in nearly every battle of his life. He rode back to camp heavy with grief. Four days later he returned to the battlefield with Red Feather, hoping to find Hump's body and bury him. "We didn't find anything but the skull and a few bones," Red Feather recalled. "Hump had been eaten by coyotes already. There weren't any Shoshonis around. When the Shoshonis found out whom they had killed, they beat it."

Soon afterward, Crazy Horse got himself into the biggest mess of his life. He had never stopped longing for Black Buffalo Woman, and it seems that she felt the same way about him. By custom, a Sioux woman had the right to leave her husband if she was unhappy and live with anyone she chose. When this happened, the divorced warrior was expected to behave decently and respect his wife's wishes. But Black Buffalo Woman's husband, No Water, was known to be jealous. Everyone felt that he would make trouble if his wife left him and moved in with Crazy Horse.

As a shirt-wearer, Crazy Horse had vowed not to cause trouble within the tribe. He was expected to put the good of the people first, even if it meant sacrificing something he wanted for himself. But he had been in love with Black Buffalo Woman for a very long time, and at some point following the death of Hump, he decided to make her his wife.

One morning while No Water was away hunting, Black Buffalo Woman left her children with some relatives and rode off with Crazy Horse at her side. When No Water returned, it did not take him long to figure out what had happened. He borrowed a revolver and went after the eloping couple. Two days later, he caught up with them at a camp on the Powder River.

Crazy Horse and Black Buffalo Woman were sitting by the fire in a friend's lodge when No Water suddenly threw back the tipi flap, burst inside, waved his pistol, and shouted, "My friend, I have come!"

Crazy Horse jumped to his feet and reached for his knife. Little Big Man, a young warrior who had been sitting next to him, grabbed his arm, trying to prevent a fight. But No Water stepped forward and fired. The bullet hit Crazy Horse just below his left nostril, followed the line of his teeth, and fractured his upper jaw. He fell forward into the fire.

No Water ran out of the lodge, jumped on his horse, and fled into the night. When he got back to his village, he told his friends that he had killed

On the left, a couple stand folded in a courting blanket. On the right, they are eloping.

Crazy Horse. They immediately built a sweat lodge for him, to help purify him of the murder.

Crazy Horse wasn't dead, but he was painfully wounded. He was carried to the lodge of an uncle, Spotted Crow, where he fell into a fitful sleep. Every so often he would stir and mumble through his broken jaw, "Let go! Let go of my arm!" Perhaps he was remembering his vision, when his arms were held by one of his own people. Black Buffalo Woman, meanwhile, returned to her relatives and asked their protection. Crazy Horse's friends searched for No Water. When they couldn't find him, they killed his favorite mule.

The incident threatened to destroy the tribal peace of the Oglalas. Crazy Horse was a member of the Hunkpatila band, while No Water belonged to the Bad Faces. The two bands had been at odds in the past, and now there was the danger of a violent blood feud. "For a while it looked as if a lot of blood would flow," He Dog recalled.

Friends and relatives of the two men went to work quietly behind the scenes, trying to keep peace between the bands. Crazy Horse could not speak clearly through his swollen jaw, but he indicated by sign language that there must be no further trouble. No Water tried to make amends, sending three of his finest ponies to Worm, Crazy Horse's father. By accepting the horses, Worm indicated that his family was satisfied and the matter was closed. Black Buffalo Woman stayed with her relatives for a time, then agreed to go back to her husband. "If it had not been settled this way, there might have been a bad fight," said He Dog.

Crazy Horse recovered slowly. His wound healed, forming a prominent scar. Meanwhile the Big Bellies—the Oglala Society of Elders—decreed that Crazy Horse had disgraced himself. He had broken his vows as a shirt-wearer, putting his personal interests ahead of the well-being of the tribe, endangering the peace of the people. He was told to return his ceremonial shirt. He could be a shirt-wearer no longer.

Several months later, Crazy Horse was out on the plains hunting when he happened to spot No Water in the distance. He jumped on his pony and chased his rival all the way to the Yellowstone River. When No Water made his horse plunge into the river and swim across, Crazy Horse did not follow him any farther.

The next day, No Water, Black Buffalo Woman, and their children packed up and left the Bad Faces camp, along with their supporters. They went south, where they joined Red Cloud at his reservation agency. No Water had nothing more to do with the Powder River Oglalas. Before long, Black Buffalo Woman gave birth to a light-haired little girl. "Many people believe this child was Crazy Horse's daughter," He Dog said, "but it was never known for certain."

Soon Crazy Horse was plunged into grief again. An Oglala hunting party returned to the village with terrible news. As the men were riding home, a band of white miners had fired on them. Suddenly many bullets came flying past. They whipped up their horses and got away, but Little Hawk was not among them. Crazy Horse was told that Little Hawk, the brother he adored, had been killed.

Little Hawk dead! Along with Hump, Little Hawk had been his best friend and closest companion. Crazy Horse had taught his younger brother everything he knew, had shared so many adventures with him. He had watched him grow into a carefree daredevil who took countless risks and was never hurt in a fight with rival Indians. Now Little Hawk was gone, killed by the bullets of some Indian-hating white men.

There were some who felt that Crazy Horse blamed himself. This awful thing had happened because he had thought of himself instead of the good of his people. And now misery had fallen on those around him, on all those who had loved the laughing Little Hawk.

10

Sitting Bull

Roaming through the Powder River country, Crazy Horse and his Oglalas mingled with their Sioux relatives in the north country, the Miniconjous, the Sans Arcs, and the Hunkpapas. Tough and resourceful, these tribes were determined to remain independent and free, and they stayed outside the boundaries of the Great Sioux Reservation. They became known to the whites as the "hunting bands" or the "hostiles."

Crazy Horse struck up a fast friendship with Sitting Bull of the Hunkpapas. The two men had very different personalities, but on the important issues of the day they saw eye to eye. Sitting Bull was several years older than Crazy Horse. A magnetic war chief, a holy man, and a spellbinding orator, he had vowed to resist any change in the Sioux way of life. Crazy Horse clearly admired Sitting Bull. And his people felt strong knowing that they had such a powerful ally.

By now, Crazy Horse had reached his thirties. The powder-blackened scar at the corner of his nose stood out against his light skin, and his hair seemed longer than ever, fur-wrapped braids hanging below his belt. As always, he dressed simply and said little as he padded about the village in his unassuming way.

His friends worried about him, for they saw how alone he was—a single man who had passed through his wild years and well into his quieter time, still living in his parents' lodge. It seems that He Dog, Spotted Crow, and Red Feather decided that Crazy Horse needed a wife. They arranged a match. Her name was Black Shawl. She was Red Feather's older sister, in her late twenties, and like Crazy Horse, still unmarried. "All I can say about [their marriage]," Red Feather recalled, "is that Crazy Horse and my sister stayed single longer than is usual among our people."

By all accounts, the marriage was a happy one. Crazy Horse and Black Shawl stayed together for the rest of their lives. Within a year, Black Shawl gave birth to a baby, whom they named They-Are-Afraid-of-Her. Crazy Horse delighted in being a father and spent hours doting on the little girl. Black Shawl's mother came to live with them. Crazy Horse was able to enjoy a warm and comfortable domestic life at last, as the laughter of a growing child and his little family brightened his lodge.

Crazy Horse and Sitting Bull joined forces during the summer of 1872, when a railroad surveying party invaded the Powder River country. Sioux scouts were watching from the hills as four hundred soldiers escorted twenty railroad workers into the valley of the Yellowstone River in Montana. The Northern Pacific Railroad was pushing westward from St. Paul, Minnesota, heading toward Seattle, Washington. Now it was about to enter territory the Sioux considered their own.

Government officials claimed that the Fort Laramie Treaty gave them the right to build railroads anywhere on the plains. On this point, the wording of the treaty was open to different interpretations, but the leaders of the hunting bands cared nothing about that. Most of them had never signed the

Crazy Horse and Sitting Bull mounted before their warriors.

treaty and knew little about its contents. They knew only that the Yellowstone and its tributaries belonged to them, land that had been gained from the Crows and Shoshonis at the cost of Sioux blood. And they knew what had happened to their southern relatives when the Union Pacific and Kansas Pacific railroads had advanced across the plains. Railroads scared off the buffalo and brought in white people. A railroad was a threat. It could not be allowed in the midst of the Powder River country.

That summer, Crazy Horse and Sitting Bull led a big war party against the railroad workers and their military escort. At daybreak on August 14, warriors attacked the soldiers' camp on the north bank of the Yellowstone, at the mouth of Arrow Creek. Indians covered the high bluffs overlooking the camp. In the valley below, other warriors galloped back and forth along a "daring line," firing arrows and bullets from horseback. Armed with carbines and plenty of ammunition, the soldiers were able to keep the Indians at a distance.

This long-range firing went on for half the morning. Then Crazy Horse made a daring move. Rifle across his lap, a bow and quiver at his back, he rode out into the valley toward the soldiers' defensive line in the thickets along the riverbank. He hoped to draw some soldiers out for a fight, and he wanted to show off his courage to Sitting Bull. Without changing his expression, he rode back and forth slowly, keeping just beyond the range of the soldiers' bullets.

Sitting Bull was watching from the bluffs. Now was the time to display his own bravery. All eyes turned toward him as he made his way down the hillside and sauntered out into the valley as though he were enjoying a leisurely stroll. He wore two feathers in his hair. He was carrying his tobacco pouch and long-stemmed pipe.

About a hundred yards beyond the Indians' line, he sat down on the grass, facing the soldiers. Then he shouted, "Any other Indians who wish to smoke with me, come on!"

Calmly he filled his pipe bowl with tobacco. Two Hunkpapa warriors, White Bull and Gets-the-Best-Of, along with two visiting Cheyennes, ventured cautiously out into the valley and sat down beside Sitting Bull. He kindled the tobacco, puffed a few times, then passed the pipe to his companions. Each man took a couple of puffs and passed the pipe quickly down the line as the soldiers' bullets sang through the air.

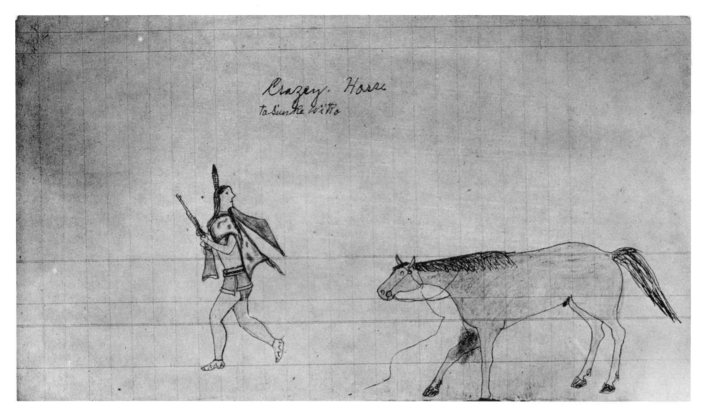

Crazey. Horse
ta Sun he witho

*Crazy Horse leaving
his wounded horse.*

"We others wasted no time," White Bull remembered. "Our hearts beat rapidly, and we smoked as fast as we could. All around us the bullets were kicking up the dust, and we could hear the bullets whining overhead. But Sitting Bull was not afraid. He just sat there quietly, looking around as if he were at home in his tent, and smoked peacefully."

When all the tobacco had burned, Sitting Bull cleaned his pipe bowl with a stick, put the pipe back into its pouch, rose lazily to his feet, and strolled back to the line of admiring warriors who had been watching his every move. It was, as White Bull remembered, "the bravest deed possible." The other smokers scrambled to their feet and ran back. Gets-the-Best-Of was so excited that he left his bow and arrows on the ground. White Bull ran back to retrieve them.

After that, Sitting Bull wanted to call off the fight, since nothing was being accomplished. "That's enough!" he shouted. "We must quit! That's enough."

But Crazy Horse could not ignore Sitting Bull's dramatic performance. He insisted on making one more dash along the daring line and asked White Bull to go with him. Armed only with a lance, he raced the length of the line, with White Bull galloping behind him as soldiers' bullets again filled the air. When Crazy Horse was nearly back to the Indians' line, a bullet struck his horse and he went tumbling to the ground. Scrambling to his feet, he ducked his head and ran the rest of the way to safety.

With that, the warriors galloped away and the Battle of Arrow Creek was over. Although the fight was a standoff, the railroad workers refused to go any farther that summer. The next day, they headed east again. The Indians had put on a show of force, a warning that they would fight to stop any railroad from coming through their country.

But the government did not intend to abandon the Northern Pacific. "This railroad is a national enterprise," General Sherman told Congress, "and we are forced to protect the men during its survey and construction, through, probably, the most warlike nation of Indians on this continent, who will fight for every foot of the line."

The following summer, railroad surveyors returned to the Yellowstone. Now they were escorted by the Seventh Cavalry Regiment, a crack Indian-fighting force commanded by Lieutenant Colonel George Armstrong Custer. Custer was a famous Civil War hero who had gone west after the war looking for adventure and glory. Fearless in battle, reckless of his own life and those of his men, he had led the Seventh Cavalry in campaigns against the Southern Cheyennes and other tribes on the southern plains.

Noting that his reddish-gold hair fell almost to the shoulders of his fringed buckskin jacket, the Indians called him "Long Hair."

Sioux warriors led by Crazy Horse and Sitting Bull fought several sharp skirmishes with Custer's troops in the Yellowstone valley during the summer of 1873. The soldiers, armed with carbines, again held the Indians off. In one fight, Custer managed to escape unhurt after his horse was shot out from under him. That year, the railroad surveyors were able to finish their work before returning east.

Several months later, Custer was back in Sioux territory, ready for another adventure. This time, he was searching for gold.

11

The Thieves' Trail

For years, rumors had circulated that rich deposits of gold were waiting to be discovered in the Black Hills—the sacred *Paha Sapa* of the Sioux, a place of mystery where game flourished, trees grew tall, and spirits dwelled. The Sioux had named these hills the *Sapa*, or Black Hills, because of their color when seen from the plains. The slopes and peaks were so heavily wooded with dark pines that the mountains, from a distance, actually did look black.

While the Sioux considered everything on earth in some way sacred, the Black Hills had a special meaning. They offered clear mountain lakes and streams, sheltered valleys, and a refuge from the storms of the plains. They were a source of scarce lodgepoles for tipis, and of secret medicine plants that healed the tribe. And they were regarded as a holy place, a place for vision quests, a home to *Wakantanka*, the Great Mystery, the sum of all that was powerful and sacred.

The Fort Laramie Treaty had promised these hills to the Sioux "so long as the grass shall grow and the waters flow." But the promise of gold proved

A symbolic drawing of the "dream elk" or "spirit elk" as it appeared in a vision.

stronger than any words. White miners were demanding that the government open the Black Hills to prospecting.

Early in 1874, General Philip H. Sheridan, commander of the Military Division of the Missouri, decided that he needed a fort in the area to keep an eye on the Sioux. He ordered his young protégé, Colonel George Custer, to explore the Black Hills. Custer set out with an expedition of 1,200 men—his Seventh Cavalry Regiment, two infantry companies, and a big group of geologists, miners, and newspaper reporters. Leading the expedition were a hundred Arikara Indians, longtime enemies of the Sioux, who had been hired by the army to serve as scouts. Few whites had ever set foot in the Black Hills. Until now the region had remained unknown and unexplored, except by the Indians who claimed *Paha Sapa* as their own.

The whites were stunned by the spectacular beauty of the place. "One of the most beautiful spots on God's green earth," wrote the reporter for the

Bismarck Tribune. "No wonder the Indians regard this as the home of the Great Spirit and guard it with such jealous care."

Custer sent back excited messages that his expedition had found what it was looking for. Gold had been discovered "from the grass roots down." Right away, prospectors stampeded into the hills, brushing past troops who made halfhearted attempts to keep them off the Indians' land.

According to the Fort Laramie Treaty, the Black Hills were part of the Great Sioux Reservation. By the time the Indians realized what was happening, however, their sacred *Paha Sapa* was swarming with gold-hungry prospectors. The Sioux began to call Long Hair Custer "The Chief of All the Thieves," and his route to the Black Hills "The Thieves' Trail."

At Red Cloud and Spotted Tail agencies, the reservation Sioux complained bitterly about the heavily armed miners who were taking over the Hills. Up north, the Powder River hunting bands did not bother to complain. They sent out war parties to harass the miners, but it soon became obvious that the whites could not be driven away. There was too much gold hidden in those hills—billions of dollars worth, as it later turned out.

Crazy Horse, meanwhile, was faced with another painful personal loss. That summer he led a raid against the Crows. On the way home, the Sioux warriors found that their village had moved. Sticks laid on the ground and signs painted on buffalo skulls pointed the way to the new encampment. As Crazy Horse approached it, he was met by his father. Worm took Crazy Horse aside and told him that his little girl had fallen ill while the war party was gone. They-Are-Afraid-of-Her had died of cholera. Her body had been left on a burial scaffold near the old encampment, about seventy miles away.

Black Shawl was in mourning. She sat grieving by the dead fire in the quiet darkness of their lodge, her hair loose and cut off, her face streaked with dirt, her arms and legs caked with dried blood where she had gashed

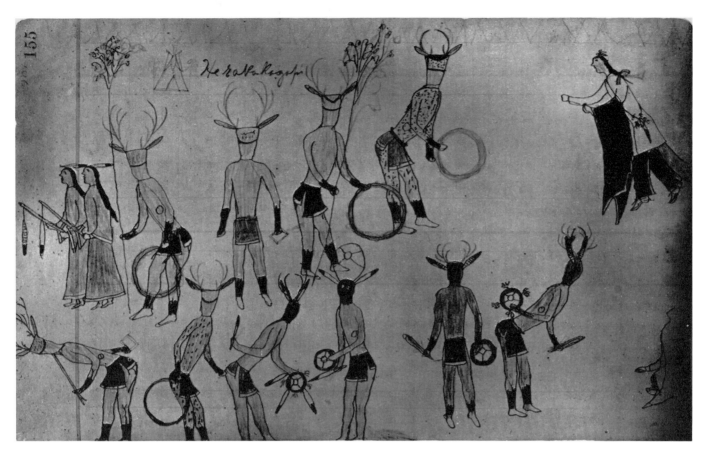

A deer dreamers' ceremony. Long-tailed deer, black-tailed deer, and elk are represented by dancers who have dreamed of these spirit creatures.

her flesh. Crazy Horse sat with her into the night. The next day he rode off to find the scaffold that held his daughter. A frontier character named Frank Grouard was living with the Oglalas at the time, and he claimed that he accompanied Crazy Horse on this sad journey.

It took them two days to reach the burial site. They found the scaffold with its little bundle at the edge of a grove of trees. According to Grouard, the child's body lay on top of the scaffold, wrapped in a red blanket. Tied to the blanket was a deerskin doll. And on the scaffold's posts hung some of the playthings that They-Are-Afraid-of-Her had loved—a rattle of antelope hooves strung on rawhide, a bouncing bladder with little stones inside, a painted willow hoop. When Crazy Horse saw all this, he could not contain his grief. He mounted the scaffold, lay facedown beside the body of his daughter, and with wracking sobs let his sorrow sweep over him.

In 1875, the United States announced that it wanted to buy the Black Hills from the Sioux. Red Cloud and Spotted Tail were again summoned to Washington, where government officials tried to persuade and pressure them to agree to a sale. President Grant himself warned that if the Sioux refused to sell, it would be difficult to keep white miners out of the hills. But the two chiefs would not be cowed. They had no authority to make such a decision, they said, and must return home to talk things over with their people.

In August, the Moon of Black Cherries, a government commission traveled to Red Cloud Agency, which was now located at a new site on the White River in Nebraska. The commissioners had come to negotiate the sale of the Black Hills. They sent runners north, inviting the leaders of the Powder River hunting bands to come down to the agency and take part in a big council of all the Sioux.

Sitting Bull replied that he had never been to a reservation agency and was not going now. "We want no white men here," he said. "The Black Hills belong to me. If the whites try to take them, I will fight." He sent word to the commissioners that he would sell no land to the white men. Picking up a pinch of dust, he added: "Not even as much as this!"

Crazy Horse also refused to attend the council. By now he was recognized as the head of his own band, made up of warriors and their families who shared his beliefs and wished to follow his leadership. "One does not sell the land on which people walk," he said. Unlike the talkative Sitting Bull, Crazy Horse spoke briefly when he spoke at all.

About four hundred warriors from the Powder River bands did ride south to observe the council and hear what the commissioners had to say. They joined about ten thousand agency Indians, representing all the Teton Sioux Tribes.

As the negotiations began, the Sioux leaders could not agree on what to do. Some chiefs were willing to give up the Black Hills in return for peace and security, but they disagreed among themselves over the price to demand. Others argued that selling the hills would never satisfy the whites. They would not be satisfied until the Sioux had given up the Powder River country as well and were confined to a narrow reservation without hunting rights anywhere. Selling the *Paha Sapa* at any price would be a disaster for the Sioux way of life, they said. No one man could be the spokesman for all the Sioux. And it seemed now that no one was willing to take the lead in front of all the people.

After several days of discussion and debate, the chiefs met with the government commissioners on September 23. A large tent had been pitched under a cottonwood tree, with a flap raised in front as an awning to provide shade. The commissioners sat on chairs under the tent flap, interpreters beside them and a troop of cavalrymen behind.

Thousands of Indians could be seen off in the distance, riding, walking about, or lounging in the hills. At noon, a great cloud of dust swirled up behind the hills as some three hundred warriors galloped over the ridge. Wearing war bonnets and carrying their weapons, they charged furiously down the hill, heading toward the commissioners as if about to attack. Just before they reached the council tent, they swerved aside and galloped around the tent, singing war songs and firing rifles into the air. Finally they formed an orderly line facing the commissioners.

Then a signal was given and another band of warriors came charging

Sioux warriors.

down from the hills. This was repeated again and again until several thousand mounted warriors had formed a vast circle surrounding the council tent. Some of the warriors were chanting:

> *The Black Hills is my land and I love it*
> *And whoever interferes*
> *Will hear this gun.*

Now the chiefs came forward—Red Cloud, Spotted Tail, and many others. They seated themselves on the ground in front of the tent, smoking and talking as the commissioners waited and the warriors milled about. The interpreters explained that the chiefs were trying to decide which of them should speak. No one seemed anxious for the honor, as some of the warriors had threatened to shoot the first chief who spoke in favor of selling the Black Hills.

Suddenly there was a big commotion. The circle of warriors parted and through the opening rode Little Big Man, the young warrior from Crazy Horse's camp. Mounted bareback on a fine iron-gray pony, he was wearing only a breechcloth and a flowing eagle's-feather war bonnet. In one hand he clutched a Winchester rifle, in the other a fistful of cartridges. Riding toward the council tent, he roared at the top of his voice, "I have come to kill the white men who are trying to steal my land."

Before Little Big Man could make another move, he was surrounded and seized by the Oglala police, reservation Indians whose job it was to keep order. They snatched his rifle, and amidst great confusion and excitement, hustled him out of the warriors' circle. Many of the warriors were riding back and forth, shouting at the commissioners, shaking their fists and weapons, bumping their ponies against the soldiers' cavalry horses, hurling insults as though they were getting ready for a fight. Some of them were yelling *Hoka Hey!* the call for a charge.

Just then, Young-Man-Afraid-of-His-Horses, who was in charge of the Indian police, rode into the center of the circle. He shouted to the warriors to go back to their lodges. "Don't return until your heads have cooled," he yelled. Young Man Afraid was respected by everyone. The warriors began to leave the area band by band, riding over the hills toward their camps.

The next day, most of the warriors from the Powder River bands left the agency and headed north again. The talks continued without them for several more days as the agency chiefs and the commissioners argued over how much the government should pay for the Black Hills, should the Indians choose to sell.

"Maybe you white people think I ask too much from the government," Red Cloud said, "but I think these hills extend clear to the sky, maybe they go above the sky, and that is the reason I ask so much. I think the Black Hills are worth more than all the wild beasts and all the tame beasts in the possession of the white people . . . but now you want to take them from me and make me poor, so I ask so much that I won't be poor."

Another chief, Spotted Bear, put it this way: "Our Great Father has a big safe and so have we. This hill is our safe."

The commissioners finally offered to purchase the Hills outright for six million dollars. The chiefs refused, saying that price was much too low. And so the council ended without accomplishing anything.

Frustrated and embarrassed, the commissioners returned to Washington. In an angry report, they blamed the breakdown of negotiations on the Sioux hunting bands, the "hostiles." The commissioners accused the Powder River Sioux of obstructing the sale of the Black Hills and violating the Fort Laramie Treaty, because they had refused to settle on the reservation and take up farming.

That ended the government's efforts to buy the Black Hills peacefully. By now, thousands of prospectors had moved openly into the hills, laid out towns, organized local governments, and demanded that troops protect them from the Indians. At Black Hills mining camps like Deadwood and Custer City, Sioux scalps commanded as much as three hundred dollars when they were sold at auction.

In November, 1875, President Grant met secretly at the White House with members of his cabinet, his military advisers, and the commissioner of Indian affairs. They agreed on a plan to deal with the troublesome hunting bands that had defied the government at every turn. The Sioux would be forced to abandon their hunting grounds in the Powder River country and move permanently to the reservation.

After the White House meeting, a government inspector issued a report intended to support the presidential decision. Describing the hunting bands as wild, hostile, and defiant, the report accused them of raiding white settlers and peaceful Indians such as the Crows. Even though this had been going on for years, the raids now became an excuse to wage war on the Sioux. "The true policy, in my judgment," the inspector concluded, "is to send troops against them in the winter, the sooner the better, and whip them into subjection."

In December, the Moon of Popping Trees, the commissioner of Indian affairs ordered all reservation agents to send runners to the Powder River country carrying an ultimatum to the hunting bands: Report to an agency by January 31, 1876, or the soldiers would march against them.

12

Soldiers Upside Down

The hunting bands didn't know what to make of the ultimatum brought by Indian messengers running through snowdrifts and bitter cold. Report to an agency by the end of January, the Moon of Frost on the Lodge?

They couldn't come in on such short notice—not in the dead of winter, when the snow was deep and the ponies too thin to travel. Maybe in the spring they would go down to the reservation agencies to trade their buffalo robes. And maybe then they could discuss their future. Anyway, this was their country. No one could tell them where to go or when.

"It was very cold," an Oglala warrior recalled, "and many of our people would have died in the snow. We were in our own country and doing no harm."

As the deadline passed, the army made plans to drive the hunting bands out of their winter camps. Early in March, the Moon of Snow Blindness, the Indians learned that soldiers were on their way. Sioux scouts had spotted ten companies of cavalry and two of infantry marching north under the command of General George Crook. They called Crook "Three Stars" because they had seen three stars on his uniform—one on each shoulder and one on his hat.

As the soldiers approached, Old Bear's band of Northern Cheyennes felt that it would be better to obey the government order and move south to Red Cloud Agency. Old Bear was camped on the west bank of the Powder, not far from Crazy Horse, and as he prepared to leave, some of Crazy Horse's people decided to join him. They were led by He Dog, who had grown up with Crazy Horse and fought beside him so many times.

He Dog told Crazy Horse that he was worried about his women and children. It would be very hard for them when the soldiers came. Many of the children were too little to run in the snow. He Dog felt that he had to protect his helpless ones, and Crazy Horse did not try to stop him.

But before He Dog and Old Bear could get on their way, Crook's scouts found their camp. An advance force of six cavalry companies launched a furious attack on the Indian village at daybreak on March 17. The temperature had dropped to forty degrees below zero that morning, and a thick ice fog hung over the snow-covered valley.

Taking the Indians by surprise, troopers on white horses charged into the village, firing their pistols as the Indians worked frantically to free themselves from their sleeping robes and break out of tipis fastened tightly against the cold. Men, women, and children ran for their lives while the soldiers used torches to set the village aflame. "From a distance we saw the destruction of our village," the Cheyenne warrior Wooden Leg remembered. "Our tipis were burned with everything in them. . . . I had nothing left but the clothing I had on."

Most of the Indians fled up a steep hillside. Once there, the warriors rallied. They counterattacked with such fury that the troops began to give way.

Shortly after noon, with four of their men dead and six wounded, the soldiers pulled out of the smoldering village and beat a rapid retreat up the Powder River to rejoin General Crook's main force.

The Indians had suffered lighter casualties, with two dead and several wounded, but most of their possessions had been destroyed, including large quantities of buffalo meat. Now they found themselves homeless and destitute in the bitter cold. Short on food, clothing, and shelter, they made their way down the Powder River for three days until they found refuge with Crazy Horse and his people.

Word of the attack on Old Bear's peaceful Cheyenne village spread quickly among the hunting bands. If the Indians had not taken the government's ultimatum seriously before, they understood now that the soldiers had declared war.

Crazy Horse led his people farther north to join forces with Sitting Bull. Hunting bands were coming in from all over the Powder River region, gathering together in one large and growing encampment. The warriors talked of striking back at the whites. And when the chiefs met in council, there was little debate. "At this great council, such as I have seen only once," related the Cheyenne chief Two Moons, "all agreed to stay together and fight."

But they also agreed not to go looking for a fight. The Indians would stay away from the soldiers if they could, but they would fight if they were attacked.

Runners were sent out to all the government agencies, calling on the reservation Indians to come north with guns and join the hunting bands. Since the signing of the Fort Laramie Treaty eight years earlier, thousands of Sioux had moved to the reservation, attracted by stories of winter handouts and the promise of an easier life. Now many of them regretted that move. As the winter snows melted, Indians began to leave the reservation and head north.

From Red Cloud, Spotted Tail, Standing Rock, and Cheyenne River agencies, Indians set out for the Powder River country. Among them were young warriors who wanted to prove their courage in battle, hunters who longed to

Moving camp.

chase the buffalo again, people of all sorts who were unhappy with reservation life and angry over the white people's attempt to seize the Black Hills. Hundreds of the newcomers were Oglalas who camped with Crazy Horse when they arrived. By the Moon of Ponies Shedding Hair, May 1876, the reservation agencies had lost half of their Indian population.

Even Red Cloud's son, Jack Red Cloud, showed up. He was carrying his father's eagle-feather war bonnet and a silver-mounted rifle that had been given to Red Cloud in Washington. However, Red Cloud himself refused to join the hostiles. He warned his followers at the agency to stay put and avoid the "big trouble" that was sure to erupt up north.

The Powder River encampment grew so large that the Indians had to pack up and move every few days to find fresh grass for the pony herd.

Thousands of people had banded together, representing all the Teton Sioux tribes, along with other tribes that had allied themselves with the Sioux. Each tribe camped in its own area, pitching its tipis in the traditional tribal circle with all the doorways facing east to welcome the light that brought the day.

As honored allies of the Sioux, the Cheyennes had first place in the circles of lodges. They were the ones who led the marches and picked out each new camping site. During a march, the columns of moving people and horses were so long, the Cheyennes would have their tipis up and their suppers eaten before the Hunkpapas, at the rear of the column, had reached the new campground.

Crazy Horse and the other war leaders knew that soldiers were marching against them, but so many Indians had joined together by now, they felt strong enough to meet any threat. People were in a festive mood as they visited back and forth among the tribal circles, staged horse races and games, and enjoyed plenty of feasting, dancing, and singing.

By the end of May, the hunting bands had crossed over to Rosebud Creek to chase buffalo and make meat for the summer. They were moving through the last great buffalo range left in the United States, and the hunting was good.

Early in June, the Moon of Making Fat, the Hunkpapas held their annual sun-dance ceremony and invited all the other tribes to attend. Sitting Bull had vowed to offer his flesh as an act of sacrifice and supplication to *Wakantanka,* the Great Mystery. After purifying himself in a sweat lodge, he entered the dance circle and performed a pipe ceremony, lighting his sacred pipe and holding it before him as an offering to the earth and the sky and the four directions. Then he sat with his back resting against the tall dance pole, his legs stretched out before him.

His adopted brother, Jumping Bull, performed the operation. Using a needle-sharp awl, he cut fifty small pieces of flesh from Sitting Bull's right arm, then fifty more from his left arm. With blood streaming down his arms, Sitting Bull began the slow, rhythmic sun-gazing dance dictated by custom, moving in a circle as he gazed at the rim of the sun and prayed. After many hours, he stopped and stood motionless, looking upward as though in a trance. Onlookers gathered around and eased him gently to the ground.

When he opened his eyes, he described the vision that had come to him. A voice had told him to fix his sight on an image just below the sun. There he had seen many soldiers and horses falling from the sky onto an Indian village below. As numerous as grasshoppers, the soldiers were falling upside down, their feet in the sky, their heads toward the earth with their hats falling off. Some of the Indians down below were upside down, too. "These soldiers do not possess ears," said the voice. "They are to die, but you are not to take their spoils."

The message was clear: Despite everything the Indians had said about wanting peace, the soldiers were coming anyway. They had no ears to hear. They would attack the Indians in their village, but as shown by the soldiers falling upside down, all of them would be killed. Some Indians would be killed, too, but the people would win a great victory. In return, they must not plunder the bodies of their enemies.

Even as Sitting Bull spoke, three columns of soldiers were advancing toward the great Indian encampment from the south, the west, and the east. On June 16, Cheyenne scouts spotted one of those columns. A force of some 1,300 men, guided by Crow and Shoshoni scouts, was marching along Rosebud Creek under General George Crook, the same Three Stars who had attacked Old Bear's village earlier that year. The Cheyennes raced home. They rode into camp howling like wolves, alerting the people to important news.

The leaders of the hunting bands held an emergency council. They decided to fight. That evening, Crazy Horse rode at the head of a huge war party, leading some 1,500 Sioux and Cheyenne warriors on a night march to meet Crook and turn back his army.

The Indians attacked the next morning at dawn, taking Crook by surprise as he camped beside the Rosebud. The soldiers were saved from disaster by Crook's Crows and Shoshonis, who threw back the first attack. After that, the battle raged all morning and well into the afternoon, breaking into hand-to-hand fights as charges and countercharges swirled across the valley.

With so much noise and confusion, smoke and dust, it was hard for anyone to make sense of the fight. "Until the sun went far toward the west there were charges back and forth," recalled Wooden Leg. "Our Indians fought and ran away, fought and ran away. The soldiers and their Indian scouts did the same. Sometimes we chased them, sometimes they chased us."

Crazy Horse was in the thick of the fighting, a figure of furious action as he rallied his warriors with the battle cry, *"Hoka Hey! Today is a good day to fight! Today is a good day to die!"* Sitting Bull was at the battle scene, too, but he was so weak from the sun dance that he could barely hold steady on his horse. He watched the action from a ridge above the valley, shouting encouragement to the warriors.

One clash involved Red Cloud's son, Jack Red Cloud. Jack was in his late teens. He had been living at Red Cloud Agency for years and had never had a chance to join a war party. He had joined the hostiles with other young men from the reservation who were anxious to win their first battle honors. But as soon as Jack rode into battle, he was dragged from his horse and found himself on foot, surrounded by Crow warriors. Recognizing him, they began to taunt him, to laugh at him, and then to whip him. They snatched off his father's war bonnet, shouting that he had no right to wear it, and seized

Jack Red Cloud retreating from Crow scouts.

Jack in a running fight with a Crow.

his father's rifle, too, laughing even harder at his pleas for mercy. Then a Sioux warrior—some say it was Crazy Horse—broke through the Crow ranks, grabbed the boy, and rode with him to safety.

Another dramatic rescue took place when a Cheyenne warrior named Comes-in-Sight lost his horse when it was killed as he was riding. As he was thrown to the ground, some Crows began to advance toward him. Just then a rider galloped forward from the Cheyenne lines and reached out a hand to Comes-in-Sight, who leaped up behind the rider and hung on as they escaped. He had been rescued by his sister, Buffalo Calf Road Woman, who

Jack being disarmed and dragged from his horse.

had joined the expedition to help with the horse herds. The Cheyennes would remember this fight as the "Battle Where the Girl Saved Her Brother."

As the battle continued through the afternoon, the Sioux and Cheyenne warriors fought with a ferocity that astonished and unnerved the army troops. Again and again, the warriors were thrown back by superior firepower. But each time they returned to the attack, charging boldly toward the soldiers with their ponies at a dead run, breaking in among the troops and knocking them from their horses in fierce hand-to-hand encounters. The warriors knew that they were fighting the same soldiers who destroyed Old Bear's peaceful village earlier that year. And they were encouraged by Sitting Bull's sun-dance vision with its promise of a great victory.

When the Sioux and Cheyenne warriors began to run out of ammunition, they broke off the engagement and rode away. It had been a costly battle. Both sides had suffered many dead and wounded.

"It was a hard fight," the Hunkpapa warrior White Bull remembered, "a really big battle." Two Moons of the Cheyennes agreed. "It was a great fight," he said, "with much smoke and dust."

Crook claimed a victory, saying that his troops had driven off the Indians. The next morning, however, short on rations and with thirty badly wounded men, he had to march back to the security of his base camp

Buffalo Calf Road Woman and her brother.

on Goose Creek, where he stayed for six weeks waiting for reinforcements.

The real victory belonged to the Indians, for they had stopped Crook's advance. They had attacked a force twice as big as their own and much better armed, inflicted serious casualties, and forced the soldiers to retreat.

They were satisfied with what they had done, but this was not the great victory foreseen by Sitting Bull. In his vision, he had seen soldiers falling right into the Indian village. That meant that the soldiers would come to them.

13

The Battle of the Little Bighorn

After the big fight on Rosebud Creek, the hunting bands moved to a new camping site in the valley of the Little Bighorn—a pleasant stream known to the Indians as the Greasy Grass. Fighting men and their families were still streaming north from the reservation, and as they arrived, the Indian village grew larger by the day.

The tribal circles sprawled for nearly three miles along the west bank of the Greasy Grass and extended half a mile inland. At the northern end of the village stood the camp circle of the Cheyennes. At the southern end were Sitting Bull's Hunkpapas. In between were the camps of Crazy Horse's Oglalas, the Miniconjous, and the Sans Arcs, with the Brulés, the Two Kettles, and the Blackfeet sharing a single camp circle. There were hundreds of lodges, thousands of people, as many as two thousand warriors—to this day, no one knows the exact numbers.

As the tribes settled into their new encampment, soldiers were closing in on them. Three Stars Crook had been knocked out of commission at Rosebud Creek, but two other columns of troops were advancing toward the Indian village. One column, commanded by Colonel John Gibbon, was moving south along the Bighorn River, heading toward the mouth of the Little Bighorn, where the Indians were believed to be camped. A second column, Colonel George Armstrong Custer and his Seventh Cavalry, was marching south along Rosebud Creek, moving parallel with Gibbon. When the columns approached the Indian village, Custer would swing westward, march overland toward the Little Bighorn, and join forces with Gibbon. They would try to trap the Indians between them.

Custer was in command of about six hundred mounted troopers armed with carbines and Colt revolvers, and thirty-five Crow and Arikara scouts. He was supremely confident. Not long before, he had turned down an offer of reinforcements from the Second Cavalry, saying they wouldn't be needed. "I could whip all the Indians on the continent with the Seventh Cavalry," he had boasted. His biggest fear was that the Indians would slip away and escape before he could find them and attack.

Following the trail of the hunting bands, Custer swung west as planned and hurried toward the Little Bighorn. On the night of June 24, 1876, he ordered a forced march. Early the next morning, his scouts climbed a tall peak in the Wolf Mountains and saw unmistakable signs of an Indian village in the distant haze. Smoke from campfires hung over the Bighorn Valley, some fifteen miles to the west. In the hills beyond, the scouts could make out an enormous pony herd, covering the earth like a vast multicolored blanket.

Custer had intended to let his men rest on June 25, but now that he had located the village, he decided he could not afford to wait. He ordered his men to move forward. He must attack as soon as possible, before the Indians could learn of his presence and get away.

A few miles short of the Little Bighorn, Custer paused and divided his command. He ordered Major Marcus A. Reno to lead three companies directly to the Little Bighorn. They would charge across the stream and attack

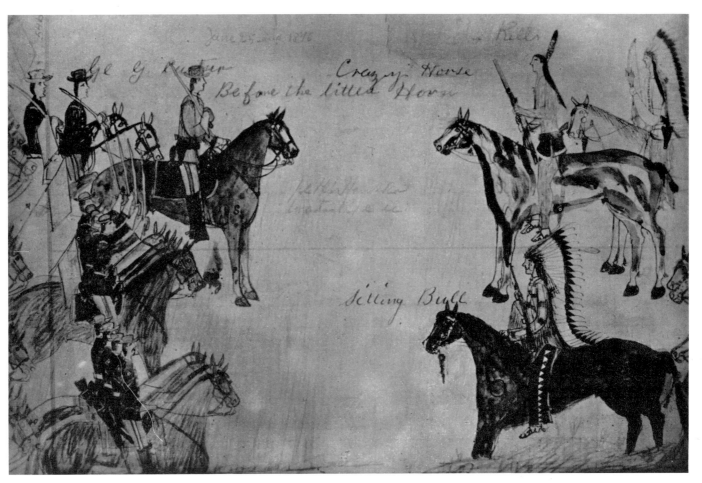

In this symbolic drawing, Custer faces Crazy Horse and Sitting Bull.

the southern end of the village. Custer himself would lead five companies along the high bluffs on the east side of the river, cross farther downstream, and attack the northern end of the village. Captain Frederick Benteen with three companies would scout south along the foot of the Wolf Mountains to make sure that no Indians escaped, then bring his men up as reinforcements.

Custer knew that the village he was about to attack was big. But he had not yet seen it, for it was still hidden to the west behind bluffs and trees. He had no idea how big it really was.

❀   ❀   ❀

The valley of the Greasy Grass offered an ideal setting for an Indian village. On the eastern edge of the valley, the river meandered clear and sparkling among thickets of cottonwood trees, gurgling over gravel and stones. Hundreds of boys and girls were splashing about in the cool waters on the morning of June 25, shouting to their friends, diving for rocks, letting themselves be swept along by the swift current.

It was another hot and cloudless day. Women gathered in sociable groups by their lodges, working on hides, gossiping and laughing. Men fussed with their weapons and smoked with their friends, and as the sun rose higher in the sky, many of the men dozed beneath the cottonwoods shading the riverbank. At the western edge of the valley, on the grassy hills, young boys watched over the gigantic pony herd. There were so many ponies, they could not possibly be counted.

Black Elk, Crazy Horse's thirteen-year-old relative, was helping to guard the horses. "Several of us boys watched our horses together until the sun was straight above and it was getting very hot," he recalled. "Then we thought we would go swimming, and my cousin said he would stay with our horses until we got back. . . . We had been in the water quite a while when my cousin came down there with the horses to give them a drink, for it was very hot now.

"Just then we heard the crier shouting in the Hunkpapa camp, which was not very far from us: 'The chargers are coming! They are charging! The chargers are coming!' Then the crier of the Oglalas shouted the same words, and we could hear the cry going from camp to camp. . . .

"Everyone was running now to catch the horses. . . . I could see a big dust

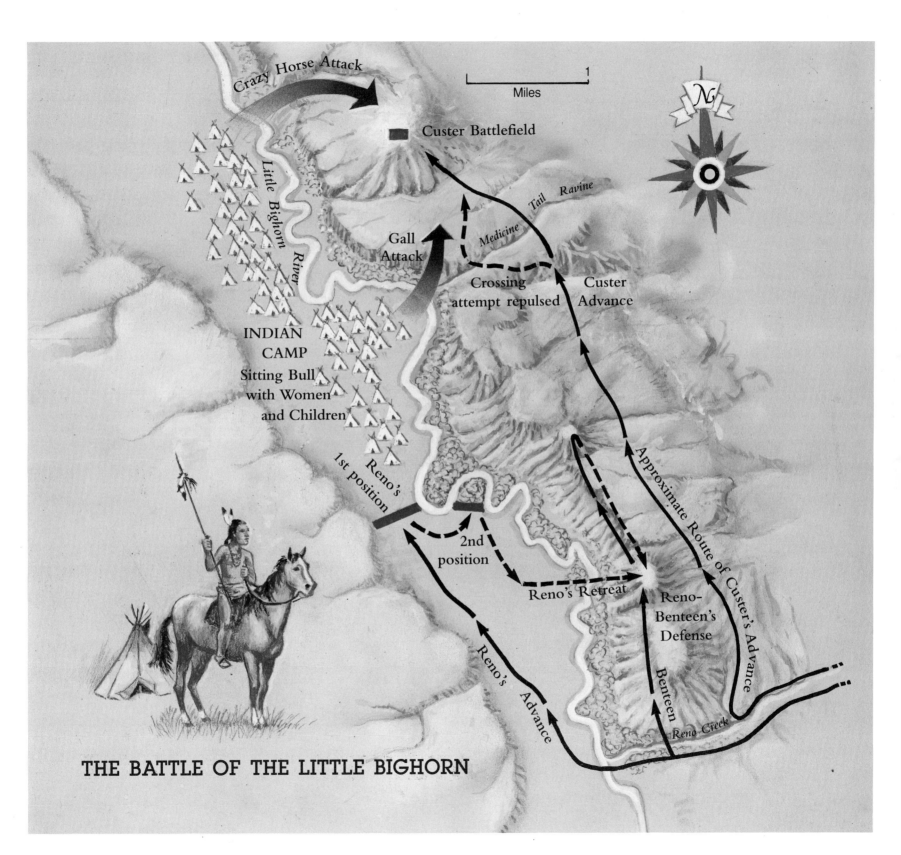

THE BATTLE OF THE LITTLE BIGHORN

rising just beyond the Hunkpapa camp and all the Hunkpapas were running around and yelling, and many were running wet from the river. Then out of the dust came the soldiers on their big horses. They looked big and strong and tall and they were all shooting."

The soldiers were Major Reno's troops. They had splashed across the Little Bighorn about two miles south of the village and were now charging up the open valley, directly toward the Hunkpapa lodges. All of the tribal circles exploded in a frenzy of activity. Warriors rushed to paint themselves for battle and get their ponies. Women and children swarmed from the river and ran for their lives.

"I heard a terrific volley of carbines," recalled Moving-Robe-Woman. "The bullets shattered the tipi poles. Women and children were running away from the gunfire. In the tumult I heard old men and women singing death songs for their warriors, who were now ready to attack the soldiers."

As Reno's troops bore down on the Hunkpapa lodges, warriors rushed out to meet them. Just short of the village, the troopers reined in their horses, dismounted, and formed a skirmish line, firing through smoke and dust at the blurred images of Indian warriors. Mounted Sioux galloped back and forth along the skirmish line, curled around the soldiers' left flank, and appeared at their rear. Reno's men held their position in the open no longer than fifteen minutes before they began to withdraw to a grove of cottonwoods along the river.

Just then a great cry went up, ringing out above the pounding of hooves, the screams of eagle-bone whistles, and the popping explosions of carbines. "Crazy Horse is coming! Crazy Horse is coming!" Mounted on his yellow pinto and shouting *"Hoka hey!"*, Crazy Horse led scores of Oglala warriors into the battle, adding new force to the Hunkpapas' counterattack.

Warriors were filtering into the woods on all sides of the soldiers, who tried to conceal themselves behind trees and in the thick brush as they returned the Indians' fire. When it looked as though the troopers would be overrun, Reno ordered a withdrawal to the steep bluffs on the other side of the river. As he gave the signal to withdraw, a bullet sang through the trees and smashed into the skull of his Arikara scout, Bloody Knife. Reno signaled again. The soldiers broke into a wild flight, galloping in full retreat across the

Reno's retreat.

open valley. Mounted warriors whooped and howled after them, knocking them from their horses with tomahawks, rifles, and whips.

A third of Reno's command was lost in the panic as the terrified troopers tried to ford the river and climb the ragged bluffs on the other side. They jumped their horses over the steep bank and floundered in the swift current as warriors kept firing at them. "With my captured rifle as a club, I knocked two of them into the floodwaters," said Wooden Leg.

Those soldiers who made it across the river scrambled up the bluffs to a flat hilltop overlooking the valley. Exhausted, they prepared to dig in and defend themselves. Just then, Captain Benteen's three companies arrived on the scene as reinforcements, and they all began to dig in together. Of Reno's 140 men who had charged down the valley an hour before, 40 had been killed, 13 wounded, and 17 stranded in the cottonwoods below.

Some warriors crossed the river, too. They were prowling the deep ravines that cut into the bluffs, shooting at the straggling troopers trying to reach their comrades on the hilltop above. Sitting Bull splashed across the river on his black horse. "Let them go," he shouted, "so they can tell the whites what happened!"

At that moment, the Indians caught a glimpse of blue columns moving along a ridge high above the river. Custer's five companies of blue-coated troopers were heading toward the north end of the village. "The word passed among the Indians like a whirlwind," said Red Horse, "and they all set out to attack this new party, leaving [Reno's] troops on the hill." Most of the warriors turned away from the hill and went charging back along the river to meet this new threat.

Custer had reached the ridge just as Major Reno began his attack. He had seen women and children running from the south end of the village and probably thought that all the Indians were fleeing in panic. He hoped to cut them off. Losing sight of Reno's men (and their wild retreat), Custer led his troops along the ridge overlooking the river, then down a long ravine that opened into the broad coulee known today as Medicine Tail. At the bottom of the coulee, Custer could ford the river and launch his own attack against the village.

Custer sent two companies galloping toward the river's bank, but they ran into heavy fire from warriors concealed in the brush on the other side. The troopers were driven back toward the bluffs after losing several men, who tumbled into the water.

At first only a handful of warriors held the ford against the cavalrymen. But they soon received help as other warriors came galloping from the battle with Reno and reached this new scene of action. Fighting men were converging on the spot from everywhere. Rallied by the Hunkpapa warrior Gall, a large party of warriors stormed across the river to meet the cavalrymen head-on. The soldiers fell back slowly, returning the Indians' fire as they retreated up the bluffs to the high ridge now known as Battle Ridge.

Crazy Horse and Sitting Bull had raced back to their camps on missions of their own. Sitting Bull and some of the tribal elders began to round up the women, children, and old folks and shepherd them to the western hills, out of harm's way. From this refuge, Sitting Bull would watch the dust and smoke of the battle roll northward along the high ridge on the other side of the river.

Crazy Horse swept through the village, rallying those warriors who had not yet made it into battle. Hundreds of fighting men were rushing about, fetching their horses, grabbing their weapons, putting on war paint. Crazy Horse led them at a gallop, picking up reinforcements as he and the others dashed through the northern end of the village, forded the river, and headed up a ravine to attack Custer.

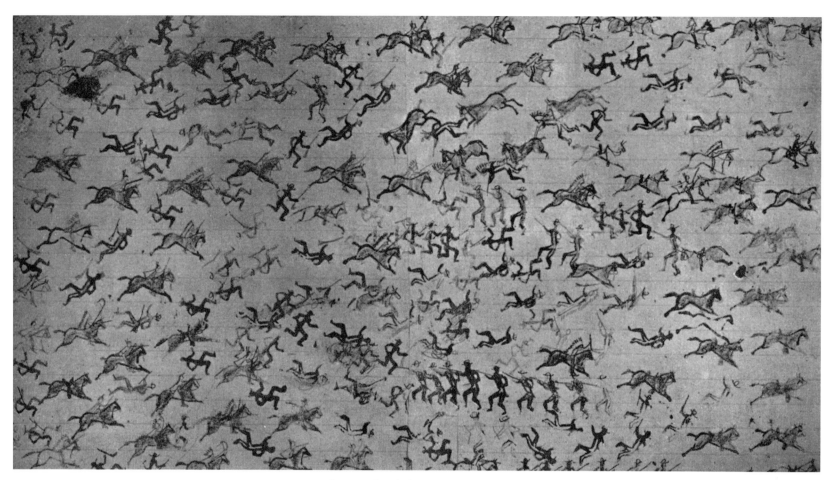

The Battle of the Little Bighorn.

"I saw him on his pinto pony leading his men across the ford," the Oglala warrior Short Bull remembered. "I saw he had the business well in hand. They rode up the draw and then there was too much dust—I could not see anymore."

Up on the high ridge, Gall's warriors were pressing the soldiers hard. As the Indians drew closer, the troopers made an organized stand. Three companies dismounted and formed a skirmish line to hold back the Indian advance.

"They fought on foot," Gall recalled. "One man held the horses while the others shot the guns. We tried to kill the holders, and then by waving blankets and shouting we scared the horses down that coulee, where the Cheyenne women caught them." The stampeding cavalry horses poured over the ridge top and galloped wildly toward the river.

By now, Custer's five companies of troopers were stretched out along the ridge. Warriors were firing bullets and arrows from behind hillocks, clumps of sagebrush, and tall grass, from hiding places in ravines. Scattered into isolated groups, soldiers fell by the dozen, then by the score. Facing disaster, Custer backed toward the hilltop at the northern end of the ridge and prepared to make a stand. He had to reach the high ground, dig in, and wait for reinforcements to rescue him.

But before he could reach the top of the hill, he was hit from the rear as hundreds of warriors led by Crazy Horse arrived on the battlefield. They appeared at the crest of the hill, their sleek painted ponies pawing the ground, snorting and frothing after the hard climb. The warriors were painted, too, and many had on war bonnets. They carried bows and fistfuls of arrows, knives and war clubs, glistening lances held high in the air. Some had carbines or pistols taken from Reno's dead in the valley, while others were armed with old trade muskets, flintlocks, and muzzle-loaders. Crazy Horse, wearing only his breechcloth and a single hawk's feather in his hair, had painted the usual lightning streak on his face and hail spots on his body.

Most of the troopers were horseless by now. Many were wounded. Hot, sweaty, dusty, thirsty, tired, and frightened, they were badly strung out along the ridge. Pressed by warriors on all sides, they fought for their lives, shooting from behind piled-up saddlebags and the bodies of dead horses.

▸▸ 1 2 3 ◂◂

Clouds of gunsmoke and dust shrouded the ridge as the soldiers tried to save themselves. Some troopers were shot down as they broke away and raced toward a deep ravine in the direction of the river. Others fell in hand-to-hand combat as the warriors charged their defenses again and again.

"The shooting was quick, quick," recalled the Cheyenne chief Two Moons, who had reached the battlefield with Crazy Horse. "Pop-pop-pop very fast. Some of the soldiers were down on their knees, some standing. The smoke was like a great cloud, and everywhere the Sioux went the dust rose like smoke. We circled all around them—swirling like water round a stone. We shoot, we ride fast, we shoot again. Soldiers drop, and horses fall on them. Soldiers in line drop, but one man rides up and down the line, all the time shooting. . . . I don't know who he was. He was a brave man."

"The dust and smoke was black as evening," said Gall. "Once in a while we could see the soldiers through the dust, and finally we charged through them with our ponies. When we had done this . . . the fight was over."

The dust settled on a ghastly scene. Long Hair Custer and every one of his men lay dead on the hillside, just short of the crest of the hill. Possibly two hours had passed from the time Reno had charged across the Little Bighorn until the last soldier fell on what is known today as Last Stand Hill.

Four miles to the south, the companies of Major Reno and Captain Benteen were still pinned down on their hilltop, surrounded by warriors who had stayed behind to harass them. The soldiers had heard the sounds of firing in the distance, but they were ignorant of the disaster that had befallen their commander and comrades. Now more warriors were returning from the fight with Custer. Armed with carbines and plenty of cartridges from the dead soldiers down the river, the Indians kept up a heavy fire on what remained of Benteen's and Reno's troops, shooting at the soldiers from all sides.

The besieged cavalrymen held off the warriors until darkness fell and the

A symbolic drawing showing the moment when the last man in Custer's command took his own life.

firing ceased. All night long they worked to reinforce their position, using knives and mess plates to dig trenches, since they had only three spades and two axes, and piling up saddles and packs as barricades. In the valley below, they could see bonfires leaping toward the night sky and hear drums, chants, and the haunting cries of families mourning their dead.

At first light the next morning, the fight resumed. From all sides the Indians poured arrows and bullets into the soldiers' hilltop defenses. Early that afternoon, Sioux scouts spotted more soldiers coming up the valley from the north — Colonel John Gibbon and his troops were on their way to join forces with Custer. Crazy Horse, Sitting Bull, and the other leaders held a council and decided that there had been enough fighting. It was time to call off the battle, break camp, and head south toward the Bighorn Mountains.

The Battle of the Little Bighorn would be remembered as the greatest military victory the Sioux and Cheyennes had ever known. Warriors defending their homes and families had fought with a passion that had overwhelmed their enemies. The soldiers had fought back with a courage that earned praise from Sitting Bull himself. At Little Bighorn, 263 soldiers were killed and 60 wounded. The Indians suffered heavy casualties also, but they carried their dead and wounded from the battlefield and never reported their losses.

"All my warriors were brave and knew no fear," Sitting Bull said later. "The soldiers who were killed were brave men, too, but they had no chance to fight or run away. They were surrounded too closely by our many warriors.... We did not go out of our own country to kill them. They came to kill us and got killed themselves."

14

Total War

Major Marcus Reno and his weary troopers watched from their embattled hilltop as the Indians broke camp and pulled out of the valley. Each band traveled as a unit with tipis packed and goods loaded, the women and children on horseback, mounted warriors guarding the line, and the great pony herds being driven along. Moving in orderly columns, the vast procession of people, ponies, and dogs wound up the slope on the west side of the valley and disappeared into the hills. As they left, Crazy Horse and other warriors set fire to the dry prairie grass, so the soldiers could not follow them.

Four nights later, at a new encampment in the Bighorn Mountains, the Indians staged a huge victory dance, celebrating their triumph. For generations to come, warriors who fought at the Little Bighorn and their children and their children's children would tell stories about the brave deeds witnessed on that hot afternoon when they wiped out Long Hair.

Sitting Bull's sun-dance vision had been fulfilled: Soldiers had fallen right into the Indians' camp and all had been killed. And yet the Hunkpapa leader was saddened because his warning not to take spoils had been forgotten. After the battle, the bodies of dead soldiers had been stripped, plundered, and mutilated. While this was customary in plains warfare, Sitting Bull worried that his people, by ignoring his vision, had invited a curse upon themselves. "For failure on your part to obey," he told them, "henceforth you shall always covet white people's belongings."

By now, the great Indian encampment had grown too big to stay together much longer. Game had been frightened away, and hunters could not find enough meat to feed so many thousands of people. One after another, the hunting bands went their separate ways, scattering through the Powder River country to hunt on their own.

Sitting Bull led most of the Hunkpapas, along with some Miniconjous and Sans Arcs, north toward the Yellowstone River. Another large group followed Crazy Horse and his Oglalas south toward the Black Hills. Many people went back to the reservation, confident that the Sioux had taught the

On the move.

army a lesson. They figured there would be no more serious fighting. From now on, they thought, they would be free to move back and forth at will from the reservation to the Powder River hunting grounds.

But the government didn't see it that way. News of the disaster at Little Bighorn had shocked and shamed the American public. Custer and all the men in his immediate command had been lost. It was the worst defeat ever suffered by the United States Army at the hands of Indians. Newspapers called for swift action to punish the hostile tribes. And government officials vowed to break the Indians' resistance. As the hunting bands scattered, they learned that soldiers were back in the field, hunting for them.

Army units called Custer's Avengers searched the Powder River country, trying to find the Indians. They had no success until a detachment of 150 cavalrymen, from a force led by General George Crook, discovered a small encampment of Miniconjous at a place called Slim Buttes, just north of the Black Hills.

Crook's cavalrymen attacked at dawn on September 9, 1876. Taken by surprise, the Indians struggled to escape from tipis fastened against a driving rain and ran into the hills. Once the warriors had placed their families out of danger, they took up positions in the hills and directed a deadly fire at the soldiers in the village below.

Runners were sent to seek help from Crazy Horse, who was camped a few miles away. He rode to the attack with about two hundred warriors. But the soldiers were well armed and held the Indians off until General Crook reached the scene with his main force of nearly two thousand men. The two sides exchanged fire for most of the day. Finally, the soldiers burned the village and marched away as Crazy Horse and his warriors harassed them. From then on, the soldiers would outnumber the Indians in every battle they fought.

Later that month, the Moon of Calves Growing Black Hair, another government commission traveled west with a new ultimatum. Congress had voted to withhold food rations on the reservation until the Indians signed an agreement on behalf of the whole Sioux nation. They must surrender all claim to the Black Hills and give up their hunting rights in the unceded territory, which included the Powder River country and the Bighorn Mountains.

According to the Fort Laramie Treaty, no new agreement could be made with the Sioux unless three-fourths of all adult males agreed. That was out of the question now, since so many Sioux men were up north with the hunting bands. The commissioners declared that the hostiles were no longer covered by the treaty. They pressured the agency chiefs to "touch the pen." If Red Cloud, Spotted Tail, and the others refused to sign, their rations would be cut off. Their people would starve. They did sign, but not until each chief had made a speech of protest. Fire Thunder held his blanket to his eyes and made his mark on the treaty blindfolded.

"Behind the commissioners, next to the wall, there was a line of army officers," Joseph Black Spotted Horse recalled. "At the door there was a company of soldiers with guns and bayonets. Farther back toward the fort, all the cannon were turned toward us. I think this was done to scare us."

Even Spotted Tail protested, accusing the government of lies and broken promises. "This war has come from robbery—from the stealing of our land," he said.

In October, the Moon of Changing Seasons, soldiers occupied all the reservation agencies. They took away the Indians' guns and horses—not just from those who had come in from the hunting bands, but from everyone, whether they had fought the soldiers or not.

Crazy Horse burned with anger when he learned that the agency chiefs had surrendered Sioux lands. In the eyes of the whites, he and his people had suddenly become outlaws in their own land. The army had declared "total war" against the hunting bands. They would be hounded and chased until they tired and gave up, submitting to military rule as prisoners of war.

That winter, army troops kept the hunting bands constantly on the move, even as snow fell and temperatures plunged. The Indians never knew when soldiers might burst into their village. "Wherever we went, the soldiers came to kill us, and it was all our own country," said Black Elk. "It was ours already when the [whites] made the treaty with Red Cloud, that said it would be ours as long as grass should grow and water flow. That was only eight winters before, and they were chasing us now because we remembered and they forgot."

One force commanded by Colonel Nelson A. Miles went after Sitting Bull. Outfitting his men with buffalo-fur overcoats and other cold-weather gear, the colonel campaigned through the hard winter months. Miles himself wore a fur cap and a long overcoat trimmed with bear fur. The Sioux named him "Bear Coat."

Miles chased Sitting Bull across Montana and fought several skirmishes with him. As the winter wore on, many of Sitting Bull's people grew weary of running. Gradually they drifted into the agencies and surrendered. But Sitting Bull and several hundred loyal followers continued to hold out, fighting back and evading capture.

Another army led by Three Stars Crook went after Crazy Horse. Before setting out, Crook declared that all warriors living at Red Cloud Agency would have to sign on as scouts and help fight Crazy Horse. When the agency chiefs objected, Crook overruled them with a wave of his hand. By promising each scout a gun and a horse, he persuaded sixty Sioux warriors to join up. One of the first to sign on was No Water, Black Buffalo Woman's jealous husband.

In November, the Moon of Falling Leaves, Crook marched north with a force of two thousand men. While searching for Crazy Horse, his scouts discovered the Cheyenne village of Dull Knife and Little Wolf. About two hundred lodges were hidden in a canyon on the Red Fork of the Powder River. In the misty dawn of November 25, Crook's cavalry pushed through snowdrifts and burst into the sleeping camp. Driven from their lodges, the warriors fought back from the surrounding hills, but their village was destroyed.

The Cheyennes lost forty men, women, and children that morning. And they lost practically everything they owned when the soldiers captured their pony herd and burned their village. Enduring terrible hardships, the survivors fled north as temperatures dropped to thirty below zero. Eleven babies froze to death in their mothers' arms. For two agonizing weeks, the Cheyennes struggled through the snow before they found refuge at Crazy Horse's camp on the Tongue River.

The Oglalas took them in and shared what little they had. "I can remember when Dull Knife came with what was left of his starving and freezing people," said Black Elk. "They had almost nothing, and some of them had died on the way. Many little babies died. We could give them clothing, but of food we could not give them much, for we were eating [our own] ponies when they died."

Frightened by the attack on Dull Knife's village, some of the Oglalas struck their tipis and set off to surrender at the agency. The others moved farther up the Tongue River, trying to stay out of the soldiers' way. By now, Crazy Horse was thinking of surrendering, too. It was a desperately hard winter that year, game was scarce, his people were hungry. The children and old folks were coughing. So was his own wife, Black Shawl. As the days grew shorter, Crazy Horse looked in the faces of his people and saw the fear and loneliness of the hunted.

In December, the Moon of Popping Trees, Three Stars Crook called off his winter campaign and went back to his headquarters at Red Cloud Agency. Instead of force, he would now rely on persuasion. He sent runners north, urging the hunting bands to come down to the agency, where they would find warm shelter and plenty of food.

Bear Coat Miles stayed out in the field. Despite the deepening snow and freezing temperatures, he continued to harass Sitting Bull. From his fort at the mouth of the Tongue River, he also sent messages to Crazy Horse, promising fair treatment if he came in and surrendered.

Later that month, Crazy Horse led his people down the Tongue. They camped almost within sight of Bear Coat's fort. Then Crazy Horse sent eight warriors riding toward the fort. They were carrying a white truce flag and leading a string of army horses that they had snatched from the fort during a raid a few weeks before.

As the Oglala warriors approached, they were spotted by Miles's Crow scouts. Before Miles could stop them, the Crows jumped on their horses and charged out of the fort, firing at the Oglalas. Five of the peace delegates were killed on the spot. The others galloped away.

Miles was furious. He took away the Crows' horses and sent them, with some tobacco and an apology, as a gift to Crazy Horse. Crazy Horse sent the horses back. Abandoning the idea of giving up, he led his people away from the fort.

Once again, the Oglalas made their way through the snow as the wind

Scouts returning with news.

howled across the frozen uplands. They camped in the most sheltered places they could find, huddling in their lodges, always ready to run from the soldiers who might attack at any time. Food was scarce, but the hunters dared not wander far for game.

Miles's troops, bundled against the cold in their fur coats, marched out of the fort and started up the Tongue River in pursuit of Crazy Horse. On New Year's Day, 1877, they found the Oglala camp hidden in a canyon at the mouth of Hanging Woman Creek. The soldiers attacked at dawn, but Crazy Horse and his warriors held them off while the women packed what they could, and the camp fled to safety.

For several days, the soldiers followed the Oglalas' trail. They attacked again and again, and each time the warriors held them off in fog and snow until the people had gotten away. On the eighth of January, the Moon of Frost on the Lodge, the two sides fought for five hours before a blizzard put an end to the running battle.

After that, Miles marched his men back to the warmth and security of their Tongue River fort. He was convinced that Crazy Horse could not hold out much longer. He must surrender or starve.

Word of a small buffalo herd drew the Oglalas farther up the Tongue to Prairie Dog Creek, in the foothills of the Bighorn Mountains. By now, most of the renegade hunting bands had gathered in this remote and sheltered valley. Black Shield and Lame Deer of the Miniconjous were there, along with Spotted Eagle and Red Bear of the Sans Arcs, and Black Moccasin and White Bull of the Cheyennes. In the middle of January, Sitting Bull and Gall reached the camp with several hundred Hunkpapas, bringing fifty cases of precious ammunition.

Sitting Bull found the hunting bands badly divided on the issue of war or peace. The chiefs held long sessions around the council fire, debating their options — to give up and save their people further suffering, or to keep fighting. The Miniconjous and Sans Arcs wanted to surrender. The Hunkpapas joined the Oglalas and Cheyennes in arguing for continued resistance. They could never accept the humiliating demand that they give up their horses and guns.

Early in February, the Moon of the Dark Red Calves, the hunting bands agreed to split up again. The Miniconjous and Sans Arcs scattered toward the east, where many of them straggled into their reservation agency to call off the war. Sitting Bull's Hunkpapas, joined by some holdout Miniconjous and Sans Arcs, headed north. They were going all the way to Canada, to the land of the Grandmother (Queen Victoria), where the Red Coats (the Northwest Mounted Police) would treat them with respect and allow them to live as they wished.

Crazy Horse's Oglalas and the Cheyennes crossed the Wolf Mountains to the Little Bighorn, where they found more buffalo. No sooner had they hunkered down in a sheltered valley than runners sent by Three Star Crook arrived from Red Cloud Agency, trying to get Crazy Horse to come in. From his fort on the Tongue River, Bear Coat Miles was also sending out runners, urging Crazy Horse to surrender to *him*. With Sitting Bull on his way to Canada, Crazy Horse, more than any other Indian leader, had come to symbolize Sioux resistance and independence. The longer he held out, the higher his prestige rose among the reservation Indians.

Crazy Horse saw the suffering of his people. He saw the despair creeping into their faces. He was tired of running. And yet the thought of surrender chilled him, for it meant exchanging the old free life of the plains for the dependent and feeble life of the agency.

"He hardly ever stayed in camp," Black Elk recalled. "People would find him out alone in the cold, and they would ask him to come home with them. . . . People wondered if he ate anything at all. Once my father found him out alone like that, and he said to my father: 'Uncle, you have noticed the way I act, but do not worry. There are caves and holes for me to live in, and out here the spirits may help me. I am making plans for the good of my people.'

"He was always a queer man, but that winter he was queerer than ever. Maybe he had seen that he would soon be dead and was thinking how to help us when he would not be with us anymore."

As spring approached, delegations of Sioux from both Red Cloud and Spotted Tail agencies were sent north to talk the Powder River holdouts into

Warriors mounted and on foot.

giving up. Red Cloud and Spotted Tail supported this effort. They believed that further suffering was pointless, and that their people on the reservation would get better treatment if all the hunting bands surrendered. The peace envoys had success with one band after another as small groups of Sioux broke away and headed south to the agencies.

"I am tired of being always on the watch for troops," explained the Hunkpapa chief Red Horse. "My wish is to get my family where they can sleep without always expecting an attack."

In March, the Moon of Snow Blindness, a delegation headed by Spotted Tail arrived at Crazy Horse's camp on the Little Bighorn. Spotted Tail carried a promise from Three Star Crook that if Crazy Horse would come in and surrender, his people could have an agency of their own in the Powder

River country, where they could live in peace. Crazy Horse stayed away from the camp during his uncle's visit. He never explained why, but he did leave a message for Spotted Tail. He said that he shook hands with his uncle, and that he would bring his people into Red Cloud Agency when the weather allowed.

In April, the Moon of New Grass, Crazy Horse and his Oglalas began their long trek down to the reservation. Lieutenant William H. Clark, the military commander at Red Cloud Agency, sent Red Cloud himself riding up-country to meet Crazy Horse and escort him in. Red Cloud set out with one hundred men and wagonloads of food and gifts.

When the two groups met on April 27, 1877, Red Cloud told Crazy Horse, "All is well, have no fear, come on in." Crazy Horse spread his blanket on the ground for Red Cloud to sit on. Then he took off the shirt he was wearing and gave it to Red Cloud as a sign that he was surrendering to his old comrade-in-arms. Ten winters before they had fought side by side to save the Powder River country. Now Red Cloud was an agency chief, doing the white men's bidding. And Crazy Horse was about to become a prisoner of war.

Crazy Horse led his people into Red Cloud Agency at noon on the sixth of May, the Moon of Ponies Shedding Hair. Thousands of Indians had gathered to watch the hostiles arrive. What they saw was a proud and solemn procession. Crazy Horse and his fellow war leaders rode abreast in the lead, carrying their weapons, their ponies and bodies painted for war. Many of them were wearing war bonnets. Crazy Horse, who had never owned a war bonnet, had his single hawk's feather in his hair. His fur-wrapped braids fell

across a plain buckskin shirt, and his Winchester rifle rested easily across his lap. His lifelong friend He Dog rode on one side of him, while Little Big Man flanked him on the other side.

Following behind, the warriors rode in tight military columns, resplendent in feathers and paint, carrying rifles, shields, bows and arrows, and lances. And behind the warriors came the village—the moving camp with the women, children, and old folks, all marching in perfect order and silence, with their travois and bundles and horses and dogs. The column was more than two miles long.

As they approached Camp Robinson, the soldiers' fort at Red Cloud Agency, Crazy Horse and his fellow war leaders began to sing the peace song of the Lakotas. The warriors behind them took up the song, and then the women and children and old folks joined in. The thousands of agency Indians lining the route began to sing, too, and to cheer Crazy Horse. An army officer watching in astonishment said, "By God, this is a triumphal march, not a surrender!"

General Crook was waiting. Crazy Horse had brought in about a thousand people, including perhaps three hundred warriors. As the warriors dismounted, soldiers stepped forward to take their horses and guns.

That same week, Sitting Bull and his followers crossed the border into Canada. The day after Crazy Horse surrendered, Bear Coat Miles captured a small camp of Miniconjous near the Tongue River. They were the last hostiles still at large in United States territory. Now there were no more Sioux in the Powder River country. The Great Sioux War was over.

15

Let Me Go, My Friends

By surrendering, Crazy Horse gave up his horse, his gun, and his freedom to wander across the plains. He became a reservation Indian, a prisoner of the army, which had never defeated him in battle. From now on, his people would depend on the government for nearly everything they needed to survive. Instead of buffalo ribs roasted over an open fire, they would eat stringy beef and flour and beans.

As soon as Crazy Horse had settled into his lodge near Camp Robinson, army officers flocked to meet him. They were intrigued by this quiet Oglala warrior who had triumphed over Custer and challenged the power and authority of the United States.

"Crazy Horse remained seated on the ground," one visitor reported, "but when [the interpreter] called his name, he looked up, arose, and gave me a hearty grasp of his hand. I saw before me a man who looked quite young, not over thirty years old [he was actually about thirty-six], five feet eight inches high, lithe and sinewy, with a scar in the face. His expression was one of quiet dignity, but morose, dogged, tenacious, and melancholy. . . . All Indians gave him a high reputation for courage and generosity. . . . He had made hundreds of friends by his charity toward the poor, as it was a point of honor with him never to keep anything for himself excepting weapons of war. I never heard an Indian mention his name save in terms of respect."

Young warriors at Red Cloud Agency idolized Crazy Horse as a hero who had brought glory to the Sioux. His prestige also was high among the army officers who showered attention upon him. They predicted that he would be as great a leader in peace as he had been in war.

It seems that Red Cloud, meanwhile, was growing envious. He had strug-

Army officers predicted that Crazy Horse would be as great a leader in peace as he had been in war: Crazy Horse at the Little Bighorn.

gled for years to come to terms with the power of the whites. And he considered himself the head of all the Oglalas. In his view, Crazy Horse had brought grief and misery down on his people by resisting so long. Now, Red Cloud began to see Crazy Horse as a rival.

No Water was one of Red Cloud's loyal supporters. He still harbored a grudge against Crazy Horse. With his friends, he began to stir up trouble for his old enemy, spreading rumors that Crazy Horse was scheming to break away from the agency and go back on the warpath. Most of the army officers at the agency dismissed these stories. Without horses and guns, how could Crazy Horse get very far? Even so, they began to watch him closely.

Crazy Horse had been promised an agency of his own in the Powder River country—or so he believed. When he asked about that promise, he was told to wait. First, army officers wanted him to travel to Washington with Red Cloud and Spotted Tail to confer with the president about the future of the Sioux. If they could persuade Crazy Horse to join the delegation, it would prove to the American public that the army had truly won the Sioux War.

"Crazy Horse wanted to have the agency established first, and then he would go to Washington," Short Bull recalled. "The officers wanted him to go to Washington first. The question of whether Crazy Horse should go to Washington before or after the site of the agency was settled upon brought on all the trouble, little by little."

Crazy Horse also had been promised that his people could go on a big buffalo hunt up in the Powder River country. But when Red Cloud heard about that, he objected. Why should Crazy Horse, a newcomer at the agency, be favored with special treatment? If he and his warriors were given horses and guns and allowed to go north for a hunt, they might never return. Spotted Tail said that he agreed with Red Cloud, and agency officials decided to call off the hunt.

By now, Crazy Horse must have been wondering if he had been wise to surrender. Shortly after he arrived at the agency, he had watched the Cheyennes being marched south against their will to Indian Territory [present-day Oklahoma]. Rumors were spreading that the Sioux were next, that they would be forced to move east to new agencies on the Missouri River, where the army would have an easier time keeping an eye on them.

When Crazy Horse finally decided that he should go to Washington after all, rumors began to fly again. Friends of Red Cloud whispered to Crazy Horse that he was in danger. The journey was a trap, they told him, for the government planned to put him in chains and ship him to an island prison off the Florida coast.

"Other Indians were jealous of him," said Little Killer, "and afraid that if he went to Washington, they would make him chief of all the Indians on the reservation. These Indians came to him and told him a lot of stories. After that he would not go there."

That summer, the army wanted to recruit Sioux scouts to help fight in a new war against the Nez Percé Indians of Idaho. The Nez Percés had broken out of their reservation and fought their way across the mountains into eastern Montana. The military commander at Red Cloud Agency, Lieutenant Clark, offered the Oglalas horses, uniforms, and new repeating rifles if they would sign on as scouts.

Crazy Horse was under great pressure to lead the scouts, but he objected. "I came here for peace," he told Clark. "You got me to come here and you can keep me here by force if you choose, but you cannot make me go anywhere that I refuse to go." When Clark persisted, Crazy Horse threatened to take his people and head north.

Crazy Horse was speaking to Clark through interpreters, and it may be that his words were twisted. The interpreters began to argue over what he

▶▶143◀◀

had actually meant to say. They exchanged angry words, and one interpreter stormed out of the meeting. It seemed to Clark that Crazy Horse was threatening to go on the warpath. By that time, Crazy Horse had had enough of talking. He, too, walked out of the meeting.

Clark and his fellow officers saw trouble brewing. The recruitment of scouts was canceled, and General Crook was summoned to Camp Robinson to straighten things out. When Crook arrived, he called a big council of all the Sioux leaders. Crazy Horse refused to attend. He told his friend He Dog that he wanted nothing to do with Three Stars Crook. "Some people over there have said too much," he said. "I don't want to talk to them anymore. No good would come of it."

While Crook was on his way to the council meeting, he was stopped by one of No Water's friends, who warned the general that Crazy Horse was plotting to kill him. Crook may have believed the story. Instead of proceeding to the council, he returned to Camp Robinson and summoned the agency chiefs to meet him there. When they arrived, Crook declared that Crazy Horse was leading all of them into trouble. It was up to them to preserve order in their own ranks. He wanted Crazy Horse arrested and brought to Camp Robinson.

On the morning of September 4, eight companies of cavalry and four hundred Indian volunteers, led by Red Cloud and other agency chiefs, set out from Camp Robinson to arrest Crazy Horse. When they reached his lodge, they found that he had fled with his wife, Black Shawl. Riding borrowed horses, the couple had headed for Spotted Tail Agency some fifty miles away, where Crazy Horse hoped to find refuge with his uncle.

Lieutenant Clark offered a two-hundred-dollar reward to the first man who captured Crazy Horse. Several warriors galloped off in pursuit, with

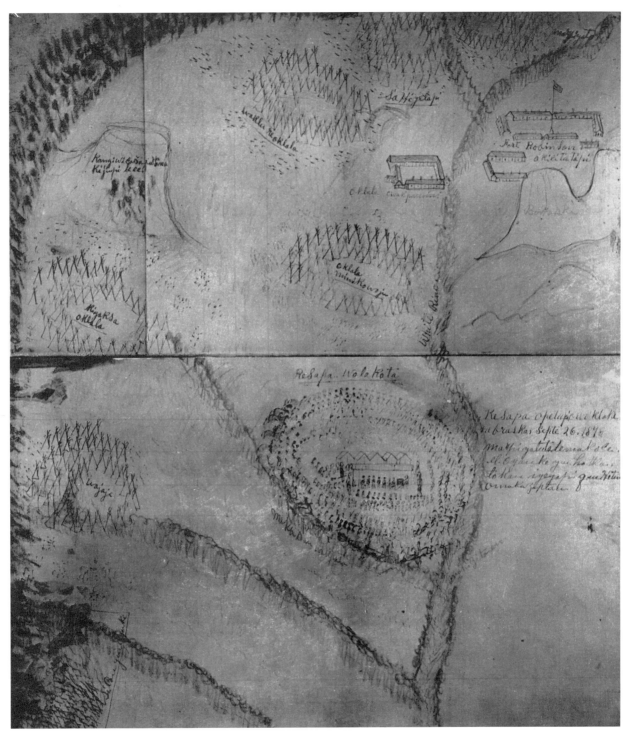

Bad Heart Bull's map of Sioux encampments at Red Cloud Agency. Camp Robinson (later Fort Robinson) is shown in the upper-right-hand corner.

No Water leading the way. It is said that he rode his horse so hard, the animal dropped dead of exhaustion.

When the Indians who were chasing Crazy Horse reached Spotted Tail Agency, they were met by Spotted Tail himself and by Touch-the-Clouds, the seven-foot-tall Miniconjou chief whose people were camping with the Brulés. After everyone had calmed down, Crazy Horse was brought out to the parade ground to show that no harm had come to him. Then Spotted Tail made a speech. Looking directly at Crazy Horse, he said: "We never have trouble here! You have come here, and you must listen to me and my people! I am chief here! We keep the peace! We, the Brulés, do this. They obey me! Every Indian who comes here must obey me!"

Crazy Horse spent the night under his uncle's protection. That evening he had a long talk with Spotted Tail, Touch-the-Clouds, and Lieutenant Jesse Lee, the local government agent. He told them that he had never threatened to go on the warpath or to kill General Crook. Those were stories spread by his enemies. He had done nothing, he said, yet a thousand armed men had been sent to arrest him.

Lieutenant Lee promised that Crazy Horse would have a chance to tell his side of the story if he agreed to return to Camp Robinson. Spotted Tail and Touch-the-Clouds offered to go with him and make sure that he received fair treatment. They also promised that Crazy Horse could move to Spotted Tail Agency and live there if that was what he wanted.

The next morning they all set off together. Spotted Tail and Touch-the-Clouds rode on either side of Crazy Horse, surrounded by Spotted Tail's warriors. Crazy Horse was wearing beaded mocassins, buckskin leggings, and a white cotton shirt. He had a red blanket wrapped around his shoulders.

By the time they reached Camp Robinson, thousands of Indians had gathered there. People were milling about, waiting to see what would happen. He Dog rode up to Crazy Horse, shook his hand, and said, "Look out—watch your step—you are going into a dangerous place."

While Crazy Horse waited, Lieutenant Lee went directly to the office of the post commander, Lieutenant Colonel Luther P. Bradley. Lee explained the promises he had made and asked Bradley to see Crazy Horse. But Bradley already had his orders from General Crook. It was too late for explanations. Crazy Horse was to be arrested and confined in the guardhouse until he could be shipped off to Omaha, and from there to some distant location where he could cause no more trouble.

Crazy Horse was still waiting when four Indian policemen came to escort him to the guardhouse. He may have thought that he was being taken in to see Colonel Bradley. Certainly he must have stared hard at one of the policemen who grabbed his arms. It was Little Big Man, who not so long before had threatened to kill the first chief who spoke for selling the Black Hills, the same Little Big Man who had fought so bravely beside Crazy Horse against Long Hair Custer and Bear Coat Miles. Now he was a blue-coated agency policeman, anxious to please the whites and rise to leadership at the agency.

The events that followed will always be uncertain. Eyewitness accounts differ, for the people who were there that day saw what they wanted to see and reported it from their personal points of view.

As Crazy Horse was being taken to the guardhouse, he must have realized what was happening. He may have caught a glimpse of other prisoners behind bars with chains on their legs. He had been promised an interview with Colonel Bradley, and now he was about to be shoved into a windowless cell no bigger than a cage.

Jerking his arms loose, he reeled around, drew a knife from under his blanket, and rushed toward the guardhouse door, slashing at anyone in his way.

Little Big Man grabbed him from behind, pinning his arms against his body. The scuffle propelled them both through the door to the yard outside.

Crazy Horse struggled to free himself as the other Indian policemen tried to wrestle him down. Soldiers standing guard rushed forward. The officer of the day shouted, "Stab him! Kill the son of a bitch!" Crazy Horse could not fight back because his arms were being held by one of his own people—just as he had seen in his vision so many years before.

A guard lunged with his bayonet and missed, driving the blade into a wooden door. He pulled the weapon free and thrust again, this time driving it deep into Crazy Horse's body.

Crazy Horse stiffened, then slumped in Little Big Man's arms. "Let me go, my friends," he said. "You have hurt me enough."

He Dog and Touch-the-Clouds both rushed up. "See where I am hurt," Crazy Horse asked. "I can feel the blood flowing."

The soldiers wanted to carry Crazy Horse back into the guardhouse, but Touch-the-Clouds stopped them. "He was a great chief," he said, "and he cannot be put into a prison." Bending down, the seven-foot-tall Miniconjou lifted Crazy Horse into his arms and carried him like a baby into the post adjutant's office. His red blanket was spread on the floor, and he lay bleeding while they sent for the post surgeon.

Outside, wild rumors were spreading. No one knew what to believe or exactly what had happened. As word spread that the warrior of the hailstones and lightning streak was dying, a hush fell over the crowd. Warriors who had fought beside Crazy Horse because they believed that freedom was more important than anything else gathered silently outside the adjutant's

office. And chiefs who had allowed jealousy to turn them against the Oglala war leader waited in shame.

His elderly parents were summoned. Worm, the old holy man of the Ogla-

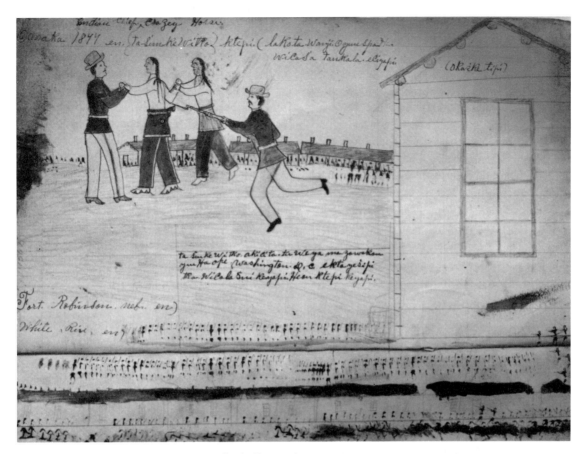

The killing of Crazy Horse.

las, entered the room and kneeled beside Crazy Horse. "Son, I am here," he said.

"Ahh-h, my father," Crazy Horse is said to have whispered, "I am badly hurt. Tell the people it is no use to depend on me anymore."

About an hour later, Touch-the-Clouds appeared on the moonlit parade ground. His giant frame was bent with grief as he announced that Crazy Horse had died. "It is well," he told the crowd. "He looked for death and it has come."

The next morning, the body of Crazy Horse was claimed by his parents. He was laid out in a simple wooden box and taken by pony-drawn travois back to Spotted Tail Agency. There the body was placed on a traditional funeral scaffold, where those who wished could come to mourn.

"No one can imagine my feelings this morning," Lieutenant Jesse Lee wrote in his diary. "I often ask myself, 'Was it treachery or not?' To the Indian mind how will it appear? My part in this transaction is to me a source of torture. . . . Crazy Horse's body was brought to this agency and put on a little platform, Indian fashion, on the hill overlooking the post, not half a mile away. Whenever I go out of my quarters I see the red blanket in which his body is wrapped, and thus is recalled to mind and heart Crazy Horse's pathetic and tragic end."

When the mourning period ended, Crazy Horse's parents took their son to an unknown burial place. Black Elk watched them leave:

"They fastened the box on a pony drag and went away alone toward the east and north. I saw the two old people going away alone with their son's body. Nobody followed them. They went all alone, and I can see them going yet. . . .

"The old people would never tell where they took the body of their son. Nobody knows today where he lies, for the old people are dead too. . . .

"It does not matter where his body lies, for it is grass. But where his spirit is, it will be good to be."

Despite bitter protests, the government had been planning to transfer the Sioux to new agencies on the Missouri River, a move urged by the generals but dreaded by the Indians. Late in the Moon of Changing Seasons, October, the forced move began. Guarded by cavalry troopers, thousands of Indians streamed eastward. All of them went reluctantly, but none more so than the two thousand "northern Sioux" who had once ridden with Crazy Horse.

About seventy-five miles east of Red Cloud Agency, there was a sudden commotion as the Crazy Horse people broke away from the column, swung to the north, and raced toward the Canadian border, bound for the camp of the exiled Sitting Bull. There were too few soldiers to stop them, so they did not try. The cavalrymen sat on their horses and watched the Indians go. They saw them disappear into the hills, heading north in search of freedom, taking the spirit of Crazy Horse with them.

About the Drawings

The old Teton Sioux had a saying: "A people without history is like wind on the buffalo grass." Deeply concerned with their past, the Sioux recorded important events by means of pictographs, or picture writing. The pictures were drawn on deerskin, buffalo, or elk hide, or later, on cloth or paper, or in the pages of ledger books. They told the stories of battles, hunts, ceremonies, buffalo stampedes, floods, fires, and all sorts of memorable happenings.

Picture histories of past events, called winter counts, were found among all the Sioux tribes and bands. Each winter, each year, was represented by a drawing of some outstanding event. The years were not numbered, but were given names, such as The Year the Sun Died (1869), when an eclipse occurred, or The Year of Heavy Snow (1852), when winter snows almost covered the tipis. Crazy Horse might have referred to his age by saying, "I was born in The Year of the Big Horse Steal (1841)." Some winter counts went back well over three hundred years.

These tribal records were kept by duly appointed band historians—a calling as honored as that of a warrior, hunter, or holy man. As a rule, each community had one historian at a time. He was expected to pick and train a successor, usually a son or nephew.

On ceremonial occasions, or when important visitors were present, the band historian would be called upon to recite the story of some great deed or testing. Unrolling his big picture skin, he would recount the event with dramatic flourish and the aid of his pictographic portrayal. "The picture is the rope that ties memory solidly to the stake of truth," was a saying of the old band historians.

Of those picture histories that have come down to us, one of the most remarkable was found almost accidentally by Helen H. Blish, a graduate student at the University of Nebraska. In 1926, while visiting the Pine Ridge Reservation in search of Indian art objects, she learned about the ledger sketchbook kept by Amos Bad Heart Bull, an Oglala Sioux. The sketchbook

Driving horses.

had been in the possession of the artist's sister, Dollie Pretty Cloud, since Amos's death in 1913. When Helen Blish first opened the worn cover of the ledger and saw Amos's drawings, she recognized his picture history as a major discovery, an important contribution to North American Indian art and ethnology.

Amos came from a long line of band historians. Born in 1869 in the Wyoming Territory, he was too young to take part in the fighting of his people during the Oglalas' last struggles against their enemies, Indian and white. As he grew up, however, he had plenty of opportunity to learn about tribal events that had taken place before his time. He was the son of a band historian, a nephew of the famous shirt-wearer He Dog, and a cousin of Crazy Horse. His father and uncles had fought against the Crows and Shoshonis, battled the United States Army, and resisted forced relocation to the reservation. He Dog and another uncle, Short Bull, had held out with the hostiles until the last.

Following family tradition, Amos sought out the stories that had made his people great. As a youth he drew a complete winter count of the Oglalas, which, in typical fashion, depicted each year by means of a pictographic drawing of a single event. So much had to be left out that he decided to begin work on a more extensive record, including ceremonies, dances, hunts, battles, tribal moves, and other significant activities. At a critical time in the life of his people, when the traditional ways were fading under the restrictions of the reservation system, he became the historian of the Oglala Sioux.

In 1890, he purchased a large ledger book and began his detailed history, eventually completing more than four hundred drawings and script notations, including sixty drawings devoted solely to the Battle of the Little Bighorn. While he developed his own personal pictographic style, he was careful to observe certain conventions of the band historian. In battle pictures, he showed the horses' tails tied up in the sign of war, but when the attack was sudden and unexpected, the tails are loose. He identified individuals not by any physical resemblance, but by showing their special equipment or dress—shield, war bonnet, bead designs, and so on.

When Amos's sister died in 1947, his ledger book, a cherished family possession, was buried with her, after the Sioux custom. Fortunately, the entire book had been photographed page by page while Helen Blish was still studying it. In the early 1930s, some thirty enlargements were made and colored by hand after the original drawings. Twenty-two of those reproductions were published in 1938 by a French firm, Editions d'Art C. Szwedzicki, in a folio entitled *Sioux Indian Painting.* All of the drawings and the complete text of Helen Blish's study were published for the first time in 1967 by the University of Nebraska Press as *A Pictographic History of the Oglala Sioux.*

Chronology

c. 1841   Crazy Horse, called Curly as a boy, born on Rapid Creek in present-day South Dakota. Differing accounts place the year of his birth anywhere from 1838 to 1845.

1851   Young Curly attends Great Fort Laramie Treaty Council at Horse Creek.

1854   Grattan Massacre, August 19. Curly sees Conquering Bear shot by soldiers under Lieutenant John Grattan. He receives powerful vision foretelling his future.

1855   Battle of Blue Water Creek, September 3. Curly rescues Yellow Woman, a Cheyenne survivor of the battle.

1857   Attends Teton Sioux council at Bear Butte.

1858   Curly's brave deeds during a horse-raiding expedition earn him the name Crazy Horse.

1864   Sand Creek Massacre, November 29.

1865   Crazy Horse joins Sioux-Cheyenne attack on Julesburg, Colorado, January 7. Acts as decoy in attack on Platte Bridge, July 25–26. Becomes shirt-wearer.

The Grass Dance.

1866–1868	Red Cloud's War: Crazy Horse leads raids against U.S. forts on Bozeman Trail. Fetterman Massacre or Battle of the Hundred Slain. Crazy Horse leads decoys at Fort Phil Kearny, December 21, 1866.
1868	Red Cloud signs Fort Laramie Treaty establishing Great Sioux Reservation and guaranteeing Sioux hunting rights in the Powder River country.

1870	Hump, Crazy Horse's best friend, killed in battle with Shoshonis.
c. 1871	Crazy Horse elopes with Black Buffalo Woman; he is shot by her husband, No Water. Little Hawk, Crazy Horse's brother, killed by white miners.
1872	Crazy Horse marries Black Shawl. Joins forces with Sitting Bull to attack Northern Pacific Railroad surveying party.
1874	Colonel George Armstrong Custer leads expedition into Black Hills. Crazy Horse's daughter, They-Are-Afraid-of-Her, dies.
1875	U.S. government tries to negotiate purchase of Black Hills. Government orders Sioux to move onto reservation.
1876	At sun-dance ceremony, Sitting Bull receives vision foretelling great Sioux victory. Sioux-Cheyenne war party attacks General George Crook's army at Rosebud Creek, June 17. Battle of the Little Bighorn, June 25; Custer and his immediate command wiped out.
1877	Colonel Nelson Miles attacks Crazy Horse's camp at Hanging Woman Creek, January 1. Crazy Horse surrenders at Camp Robinson (now Fort Robinson), Red Cloud Agency, May 6. Crazy Horse dies after receiving bayonet wound in back, September 5.

In Search of Crazy Horse
A Selective Bibliography

Much of what we know about the personal life and character of Crazy Horse is based on interviews with his surviving relatives and fellow warriors conducted by Eleanor Hinman and Mari Sandoz on the Pine Ridge Reservation in 1930. "I want their stories to go on record in their own words," wrote Hinman, "so that any student of Indian or frontier history who digs deeply enough into the materials may find them." Before these interviews were recorded, published sources on the life of Crazy Horse were almost exclusively the accounts of the white men who fought against him. See Eleanor H. Hinman, "Oglala Sources on the Life of Crazy Horse," (*Nebraska History*; vol. 57, no. 1, 1976).

Mari Sandoz used those interviews as her starting point when she set out to reconstruct the life of Crazy Horse from the dust of history. She also drew on interviews with settlers and Indians in the celebrated Ricker Collection at the Nebraska State Historical Society, on records at the Indian Bureau and the Adjutant General's Office in Washington, D.C., and on her own experiences as a young girl growing up on a Nebraska homestead in Crazy Horse country. Sandoz wanted to tell her story from an Indian perspective, reflecting the rich oral tradition of the Lakotas, so it would read like a tale told around an Oglala campfire. Viewing her character and his times through a literary lens, she built her account on imagined dialogue and dramatized scenes. Despite these fictional embroideries, her pioneering biography, the first on Crazy Horse, rests on a solid foundation of authenticated fact. A half-century after its first publication, her book remains an indispensable source for any student of Crazy Horse: Mari Sandoz, *Crazy Horse: The Strange Man of the Oglalas* (New York: Alfred A. Knopf, 1942).

The most authoritative and complete standard biography is Stephen E. Ambrose's *Crazy Horse and Custer: The Parallel Lives of Two American Warriors*

Sioux warrior.

(Garden City, N.Y.: Doubleday, 1975). In his acknowledgments, Ambrose singles out Hinman and Sandoz as among the authors and researchers who made his own book possible.

Other significant biographical works that bear on the life and times of Crazy Horse include Evan S. Connell's *Son of the Morning Star: Custer and the Little Bighorn* (San Francisco: North Point Press, 1984), Alvin M. Josephy's *The Patriot Chiefs: A Chronicle of American Indian Resistance* (New York: The Viking Press, 1961), and Robert M. Utley's *The Lance and the Shield: The Life and Times of Sitting Bull* (New York: Henry Holt, 1993).

Two unusual books deal specifically with the death of Crazy Horse: *The Killing of Chief Crazy Horse: Three Eyewitness Views by the Indian, Chief He Dog, the Indian-White, William Garnett, and the White Doctor, Valentine McGillycuddy*, edited with an introduction by Robert A. Clark (Lincoln: University of Nebraska Press, 1988), and *To Kill an Eagle: Indian Views on the Last Days of Crazy Horse*, edited with commentary by Edward Kadlecek and Mabell Kadlecek (Boulder, Colo.: Johnson Books, 1981).

The Battle of the Little Bighorn has inspired a vast body of literature. Robert M. Utley's National Park Handbook, *Custer Battlefield: A History and Guide to the Battle of the Little Bighorn* (Washington, D.C.: National Park Service, 1987), offers a compact, informative, and balanced account. The Indians' own descriptions of the battle are collected in Leslie Tillett's *Wind on the Buffalo Grass: Native American Artist-Historians* (New York: Da Capo Press, 1976), which includes interviews, drawings, and paintings. Another noteworthy account is Mari Sandoz's *The Battle of the Little Bighorn* (Philadelphia: J. B. Lippincott, 1966).

For background about the Teton Sioux, their culture, customs, and history, the following are especially useful: Royal B. Hassrick's *The Sioux: Life and Customs of a Warrior Society* (Norman: University of Oklahoma Press, 1964),

George E. Hyde's *Red Cloud's Folk: A History of the Oglala Sioux Indians* (Norman: University of Oklahoma Press, 1937, revised edition 1957), Edward Lazarus's *Black Hills/White Justice: The Sioux Nation Versus the United States, 1775 to the Present* (New York: HarperCollins, 1991), and Mari Sandoz's slim but evocative *These Were the Sioux* (New York: Hastings House, 1961).

General histories of Indian-white relations during the time of Crazy Horse include Ralph K. Andrist's *The Long Death: The Last Days of the Plains Indians* (New York: Macmillan, 1964), Dee Brown's *Bury My Heart at Wounded Knee: An Indian History of the American West* (New York: Holt, Rinehart, and Winston, 1970), Angie Debo's *A History of the Indians of the United States* (Norman: University of Oklahoma Press, 1970), and Robert M. Utley's *The Indian Frontier of the American West, 1846–1890* (Albuquerque: University of New Mexico Press, 1984).

Two acknowledged classics offer unique insights into the life and customs of the Oglala Sioux from widely different perspectives: Francis Parkman's *The Oregon Trail,* originally published in 1849 (New York: Penguin Books, 1982), and John G. Neihardt's *Black Elk Speaks: Being the Life Story of a Holy Man of the Oglala Sioux* (Lincoln: University of Nebraska Press, 1961).

Acknowledgments

I am indebted to each of the authors mentioned in my bibliography, and particularly to Eleanor Hinman, Mari Sandoz, and Stephen E. Ambrose for information and insights that inform my own account of Crazy Horse. My thanks also to the following people for helpful suggestions, advice, and encouragement: Deborah Conyers; John August Doerner, Division of Interpretation, Little Bighorn Battlefield National Monument; Gilbert Douville, Library Manager, Prairie Edge, Rapid City, South Dakota; James L. Kormier; David Lavender; Virginia Driving Hawk Sneve.

The drawings by Amos Bad Heart Bull are from *A Pictographic History of the Oglala Sioux*, by Amos Bad Heart Bull, text by Helen H. Blish, and are used by permission of the University of Nebraska Press. Copyright © 1967 by the University of Nebraska Press. Copyright © renewed 1995 by the University of Nebraska Press.

Thanks to George Buctel for designing the maps on pages 6–7, 61, and 117.

Index

(Italicized numbers indicate pages with photos)